T0323706

Cambridge Elements

Elements in Ancient Philosophy
edited by
James Warren
University of Cambridge

THE HEDONISM OF EUDOXUS OF CNIDUS

Richard Davies
University of Bergamo

CAMBRIDGE
UNIVERSITY PRESS

Shaftesbury Road, Cambridge CB2 8EA, United Kingdom

One Liberty Plaza, 20th Floor, New York, NY 10006, USA

477 Williamstown Road, Port Melbourne, VIC 3207, Australia

314–321, 3rd Floor, Plot 3, Splendor Forum, Jasola District Centre,
New Delhi – 110025, India

103 Penang Road, #05–06/07, Visioncrest Commercial, Singapore 238467

Cambridge University Press is part of Cambridge University Press & Assessment,
a department of the University of Cambridge.

We share the University's mission to contribute to society through the pursuit of
education, learning and research at the highest international levels of excellence.

www.cambridge.org
Information on this title: www.cambridge.org/9781009462600

DOI: 10.1017/9781009321532

First published 2023

A catalogue record for this publication is available from the British Library

ISBN 978-1-009-46260-0 Hardback
ISBN 978-1-009-32151-8 Paperback
ISSN 2631-4118 (online)
ISSN 2631-410X (print)

The Hedonism of Eudoxus of Cnidus

Elements in Ancient Philosophy

DOI: 10.1017/9781009321532
First published online: November 2023

Richard Davies
University of Bergamo

Author for correspondence: Richard Davies, richard.davies@unibg.it

Abstract: Mathematician and astronomer Eudoxus of Cnidus was a younger contemporary of Plato and an older contemporary of Aristotle, on both of whom he exerted some influence during his stays in Athens. This is perhaps most apparent with regard to his ethical doctrine that identifies the good as pleasure (hedonism). While Plato seems rather unsure how seriously to take this proposal, Aristotle provides the materials for reconstructing the battery of ingenious arguments that Eudoxus brought forward in its defence. Taken together in this Element, these arguments foreshadow almost everything that has been said in the Western tradition in favour of the positive value of pleasure, and, if taken aright, point in the direction of a hedonism that sets store by the cultivation of activities akin to those for which Eudoxus has been most renowned: mathematics and astronomy.

Keywords: Eudoxus of Cnidus, Aristotle, ethics, pleasure, hedonism

ISBNs: 9781009462600 (HB), 9781009321518 (PB), 9781009321532 (OC)
ISSNs: 2631-4118 (online), 2631-410X (print)

Contents

1 Eudoxus: Who He?

1.1 *'Tempore Eudoxi'*

The Cnidus (or Knidos) that gives Eudoxus his toponym was a city on what is now the southern coast of Turkey. Standing at the head of an isthmus, Cnidus was a flourishing seaport with two harbours and was colonised by astute Spartans at an early date. In 394 BCE, a decisive naval battle nearby saw the city pass under Athens' control. It may be that Eudoxus' father was prominent in the previous regime, and fell on hard times when the Athenians took over, which might explain why Eudoxus had to lodge in Piraeus when he first visited Athens (Diogenes Laertius, *Lives* (hereinafter DL), VIII.86).

We do not know for sure the date of either the birth or the death of Eudoxus. Diogenes tells us that he died in his fifty-third year (i.e. aged fifty-two) and that his *acme* was in the 103rd Olympiad (360–4 BCE) (VIII.90). But this is not a helpful guide, not least because Diogenes' source, Apollodorus, elsewhere uses '*acme*' to mean the culminating period of a philosopher's thinking, which in the case of Anaximander may have been when he was 64 (II.2). A more common usage of the word seems to have indicated an age of about forty, but it is also a commonplace that mathematicians do their best work when young.

Though some suggest that Eudoxus was born between 395 and 390 BCE and, so, would have died between 343 and 337, a more consensual dating is that he was born in 408/9 BCE. Diogenes reports (VIII.86) that Eudoxus was twenty-three when he first visited Athens, and we shall suggest in the next section that he was around the Academy while Plato was composing the *Protagoras* in about 380. If so, we might hazard that he was born in 403 and so died around 350. If so, he was twenty-four years younger than Plato (427–347) and twenty-one years older than Aristotle (384–322). Such a speculation places him almost too neatly in a generation intermediate between Plato and Aristotle to be true. It may be true all the same, but nothing much hangs on it.

Young Eudoxus headed for Athens attracted by the fame of the 'Socratics' (VIII.86) and Diogenes names Archytas of Tarentum as his teacher in geometry (VIII.86; also Iambl., *In Nic. Arith.*, 10, 17), but it remains unclear where or when they might have met, though Archytas was an admired friend of Plato (DL, VIII.79–81). It is at least as likely that Eudoxus sought out not only Socrates' followers Xenophon and Antisthenes of Athens, but more particularly the mathematicians in the Academy such as Theaetetus, who worked on irrational numbers and should be credited with individuating the 'Platonic Solids', and Theodorus of Cyrene. After just two, presumably quite intense, months in Athens, Eudoxus returned home.

Though they do not agree on the sequence of his subsequent travels, our two main sources for Eudoxus' life, Diogenes Laertius and Flavius Philostratus (*Lives of the Sophists*, I.i), agree that he spent some considerable time in Egypt, specifically at Memphis, where he adopted the rather disquieting priestly custom of shaving not only his beard but also his eyebrows (DL VIII.87) as well as learning to read hieroglyphics (De Santillana 1940, esp. pp. 255–7; also Gwyn Griffiths 1965), so that Plutarch cites him as an authority on things Egyptian (*Is. et Os.*, 353 C, 359B, 372D, 377A). Closer to his home, at some point Eudoxus visited Mausolus (DL VIII.87), who was satrap at Halicarnassus and whose tomb gives us the word 'mausoleum'. Probably around the middle of the 370s, Eudoxus moved to the wealthy city of Cyzicus on the sea of Marmara, where he set himself to teaching (DL, VIII.88: *sophisteuon*), though quite what he taught and for how long, we do not know. But it seems to have been from here, and taking a band of his students with him, that Eudoxus returned to Athens at some point before about 367–6 BCE.

This *terminus ante quem* is justified by an admittedly late and anonymous life of Aristotle (Lasserre, T6a and T6b), according to which Eudoxus was present in the Academy when Aristotle arrived there. Given that Plato was away from Athens on one of his fruitless missions to Sicily in 367–5, the phrase *'tempore Eudoxi'* ('in the time of Eudoxus') in T6b has given rise to some speculation that Eudoxus had some role as stand-in scholarch (e.g. Merlan 1960, p. 100; Fermani 2008, p. 950 n. 43; and Zanatta 2008, pp. 8–10). Eudoxus' reputation may have been a factor in Aristotle's transfer to Athens, and he was, off (DL, VIII.87) and on (VIII.88), a friend and companion of Plato. But he does not figure in the standard list of Plato's pupils (III.46) and so was not a likely candidate for such a role. Being relatively young, more interested in mathematics than in philosophical speculation and not an Athenian citizen, he would have been an unsuitable legal representative of the school.

It is not given to us to know how long Eudoxus' second stay in Athens lasted. Most of the rest of the present Element is given over to insinuating that it was long enough for him to make quite an impact on Aristotle, not a man easily bowled over. While Diogenes tells us that Eudoxus returned to his native Cnidus, where he was esteemed and commissioned to frame a legal code for the city (VIII.88), an alternative story is that, from Athens, he went back to his school in Cyzicus (Cajori 1906, p. 32) and that the school itself kept going into the third century (Taub 1998, p. 452). These versions are, of course, compatible; but Eudoxus can have died in no more than one of the cities named. We know not which.

1.2 Eudoxus' Scientific Interests

In the first lines of his account of Eudoxus, Diogenes characterises him as 'an astronomer, a geometer, a doctor and a legislator' (VIII.86). And, a little further down, he reports Hermippus of Smyrna referring to Eudoxus' studies in astronomy and geometry (VIII.88), and Eratosthenes of Cyrene ascribing to him two writings 'Against Baton' and a 'Dialogue of the Dogs' (VIII.89), about whose contents it would be fruitless to speculate. In between, apparently citing Nicomachus, son of Aristotle, but presumably meaning Aristotle's *Nicomachean Ethics*, Diogenes attributes to Eudoxus the view that pleasure is the good (VIII.88); this is the view that we shall be calling 'hedonism'. Because of his interests in mathematical questions, Diogenes places his life of Eudoxus at the end of the book devoted to Pythagoras and his followers. On the other hand, given his off-and-on relations with the Academy, some ancient writers, such as Strabo (Lasserre T13) and Plutarch (*Adv. Colot.* 1126d), associate him more closely with Plato's school; likewise some more recent commentary (e.g. Guthrie 1978, V, pp. 447–56; Reale 2004, III, pp. 456–9).

Over the last two and a half millennia, Eudoxus' views in astronomy and geometry have attracted more attention than his other activities. Even after they were overtaken or overturned as contributions to the best scientific theories to be had, they continued to hold a certain interest for historians of ancient science: of the forty studies devoted to Eudoxus logged in the *Année Philologique* for the last two decades of the twentieth century, thirty-eight discuss astronomy or geometry; one is a note on geography and one a textual point. Moreover, there is some sense in which the views he proposed are ingenious elaborations of what most people take for granted most of the time.

If, for instance, we are watching a sunset, we find it almost impossible to think of ourselves as going backwards relative to what we see. Because we feel no movement in ourselves, we attribute movement to the Sun. What Eudoxus saw, and tried to respond to, was the need for some account of these observed motions. In particular, the retrograde paths traced by the planets (literally 'the wandering ones') called for some complication of the 'intuitive' picture. Eudoxus' response was to posit twenty-seven spheres centred on the Earth carrying the heavenly bodies and interacting with each other to produce these effects. His scheme (as carried by Lasserre D6–17 and F1–272) was passed down, with amendments and elaborations, through Aristotle's *Metaphysics* (XII.8) into the synthesis of ancient astronomy that is Ptolemy's *Almagest*. The basic picture and, in particular, the mathematising approach based on circular motions remained dominant for nearly 2,000 years in Europe, until some moment between Nicolaus Copernicus' *De revolutionibus* (1543) and the multiple empirical verifications of stellar parallax in 1837, with a tipping point not long after Johannes Kepler's *Epitome* (1618–21) or Galileo Galilei's *Massimi sistemi* (1632).

If Trumpton is two miles east of Camberwick Green and two miles north of Chigley, and Winkstead Hall is two miles south of Camberwick Green and two miles east of Chigley, one might wonder *exactly* how far Trumpton is from Winkstead Hall. Or if I rotate a yardstick around a fixed point, I can be sure that the radius of the circle I have described is one yard, but I might wonder *exactly* how long the circumference is. The Pythagoreans are credited with having discerned that exactitude is not to be had in such cases: the values of both √2 and π can only be approximated. To respond to this embarrassment, Eudoxus developed techniques for successively closer approximations that were taken up and adapted into the synthesis of ancient geometry that is Euclid's *Elements* (especially Book V) and elsewhere (as carried by Lasserre D18–66). The overall Euclidean theory of space as homogeneously three-dimensional dominated European geometry until some time after Giovanni Giacomo Saccheri's self-defeating *Euclides [. . .] vindicatus* (1733) or Nikolai Ivanovich Lobachevsky's *Theorie der Parallellinien* (1840), and was given a death-blow by Einstein's 1905 and 1916 papers on special and general relativity.

Though the foregoing are caricatures, they may suffice to indicate two points. One is that, for all their ingenuity, Eudoxus' contributions to astronomy and geometry must be counted as having been superseded. These are sciences that are, in one way or another, 'progressive' and Eudoxus has been left behind. The other is that we are dependent on second-hand sources for Eudoxus' opinions, with all the accretions, interpretations and corrections that accumulate in such passages.

While the second point applies in full to Eudoxus' claim that pleasure is the good, things are more complicated with regard to the first. For, the question of the relations between pleasure and the good has not been resolved. Eudoxus' view has not been refuted, but nor has it been vindicated. So our overall aim in this volume is to try to see what can be made of the various arguments that he adduces in favour of his claim. One approach to this end is to analyse the textual evidence at our disposal with a view to reconstructing his argumentative strategies; and there are some passages in what follows in which we attempt this sort of philological explication. But, bearing in mind that we do not have Eudoxus' *ipsissima verba*, we cannot be sure how faithful are the reports we have of his views. So our dominant mode is rather more philosophical: what *must* Eudoxus have been up to in defending his claim in the ways he does?

1.3 Five or Six Arguments for Hedonism

Our underlying expository choice for setting out Eudoxus' arguments in favour of the doctrine of hedonism is to take Aristotle's *Nicomachean Ethics* (*EN*) as our leading text. This is not so much because it is a better source for Aristotle's ethical thinking than the *Eudemian Ethics* (*EE*), a view that has been contested at least since Kenny (1978), as because it is still easier to find versions of it in circulation and because it cites Eudoxus twice by name, which *EE* does not. Moreover, *EE* does not contemplate an extended discussion of pleasure corresponding to *EN* X, which will be our leading source.

A further expository device is to adopt more-or-less traditional labels for the arguments we find associated with Eudoxus in *EN* (Guthrie 1978, pp. 453–4; Gosling and Taylor 1982, pp. 255–83; Brunschwig 1986; Berti 1994; Aufderheide 2021, pp. 195–8). We list them here in telegraphic form in the order in which they first break the surface in the text of *EN*, though we shall see that some are treated more than once:

Cradle: All animate beings both rational and irrational are borne towards pleasure; that to which all animate beings are borne is the good;

Honour: Pleasure is not praised because we appeal to pleasure to praise other things: it provides some measure of their value;

Witness: Eudoxus was a man of exceptional moderation and would have proposed the theory that pleasure is the good only if the theory were true;

Addition: Pleasure increases the good of a good activity; only a good added to a good can increase it;

Opposites: Pleasure is the opposite of a recognised evil, pain; the opposite of an evil is a good; and

End: Pleasure is chosen for itself and not in view of anything else.

This order of appearance is a mere artefact of how the various considerations fit into Aristotle's argumentation. Although there are sustained discussions of pleasure in *EN* VII and X, Aristotle does not set out Eudoxus' views systematically, but uses them for his own dialectical purposes (Weiss 1979). What Aristotle knew of Eudoxus' views may be the upshot of conversations with him around the Academy, rather than of any articulated text that Eudoxus may have composed on the matter. For this reason, and contrary to a certain commentarial tradition (most recently Aufderheide 2020), we see no reason to be constrained by the order of exposition in Aristotle's most sustained engagement with Eudoxus in X.2. In any case, *Witness* is not a consideration that Eudoxus himself could reasonably have proposed in favour of his own doctrine, but pops up as an aside in the midst of Aristotle's exposition in that chapter (1172b13–18). For this reason, we shall see what it comes to in Section 3, before turning to the others.

Aristotle is overall pretty positive about the arguments to be considered. His attitude is not only that there is some association to be made between pleasure and the good, but that Eudoxus made a good fist of bringing aspects of this to the fore. Yet he tries to keep a certain distance from a full-blown doctrine that deserves the name of hedonism. Moreover, it is not clear that the various arguments all point to quite the same conclusion, and there may be tensions among them. For instance, the temperance of Eudoxus cited in *Witness* may be at odds with the appeal to irrational animate beings in *Cradle*, because irrational beings are taken to be incapable of temperance. Again, the pleasure invoked in *Addition* need not be an experience, while *Cradle*, *Honour* and *End* appear to have to do with what it feels like to have a pleasure.

After considering *Witness*, we propose to discuss the other five arguments in ascending order of the generality and exclusivity of the versions of hedonism that each is meant to support. Because *Addition* does not seek to establish much more than that pleasure is *a* good, it is the most modest and so a good place to start. Though *Honour* presupposes a hierarchy of goods with pleasure in the top rank, it does not even aim to show that pleasure is unique in this position. *Opposites* presents the negative consideration of the badness of pain to argue that pleasure is prominent among the most choiceworthy of things. On what we take to be Aristotle's view, the teleology of natural inclinations invoked in *Cradle* indicates that what is most choiceworthy is the highest good. Finally, *End* proposes a regress argument that places pleasure as our ultimate objective.

If, at each stage in this ascending order, we can make out a case for Eudoxus' doctrine, by the end of Section 7, the cumulative effect should be that hedonism is a doctrine worth taking seriously. If we reversed the expository order, starting with the strongest thesis, the appeal to Eudoxus' good character in *Witness* would seem neither here nor there, given that most theories of value have had virtuous advocates, while hedonism has generally been associated with degenerates and perverts. In this respect, our choice of overall structure for the following sections is meant to stack the odds in Eudoxus' favour.

2 Two Anonymous Appearances in Plato

2.1 The Measure of Pleasure in the *Protagoras*

In the whole of what is known as the *Corpus Platonicum*, the name 'Eudoxus' appears just once, in the thirteenth letter (360c3), where the author recommends Helicon of Cyzicus as knowledgeable about Eudoxus' teachings. Given that Eudoxus held a school in Helicon's home city, this may be true, but the author of this letter was pretty certainly not Plato himself. Even if he does not appear by name, Eudoxus seems to have been on Plato's mind in one relatively early dialogue, the *Protagoras*, and one fairly late one, the *Philebus*. Our suggestion is that this timing may correspond to Eudoxus' two visits to Athens.

There are, incidentally, two key passages in the *Republic* with a hedonistic flavour. One is the claim that joy and harmless pleasures (*Resp.* II 357b6–7: *hēdonai ablabeis*; cf. *Tim.* 59d1) are unique in being desired only for themselves. The other is the polemic in books VIII and IX, in which cognates of 'pleasure' occur about sixty times as denoting a positive factor, and that leads to the mind-boggling conclusion that the well-ordered life of the ruler of the well-ordered state will be 729 times more pleasurable (*Resp.* IX 587e3: *hēdion*) than that of the tyrant at the dissolution of society. Though the former of these considerations is analogous to our *End*, the latter is part and parcel of Plato's soul-city analogy and has nothing to do with Eudoxus. But, from the thrashings meted out to Thrasymachus in *Republic* I and to Callicles in the *Gorgias* (494a–503d), each, in his own way, a proponent of untrammelled desire-satisfaction, we may safely say that Plato was at the very least very suspicious of hedonism as a doctrine.

We are allowed (Brandwood 1992, p. 112), but not required (Denyer 2008, p. 175), to suppose that Plato was composing the *Protagoras* around 380 BCE, the date we have already insinuated for Eudoxus' arrival in Athens. We do not know for sure what Plato's compositional habits were, but it is not wild to imagine that many of the voices we hear in the dialogues echo things that were said in discussions around the Academy. One of the themes in play was the possibility of there being a science (*technē*) of pleasure, with Plato's nephew Speusippus taking the view that there couldn't be, because pleasure is indeterminate (*aoristē*; cf. *EN* X, iii, 1173a17). Indeed, as we shall see in considering *Opposites*, Speusippus maintained the even stronger thesis that pleasure is not even a good. In any case, the lines of thought pursued in the *Protagoras* are a pretty sure sign that pleasure and the possibility of a science of pleasure were hot topics in the Academy, and it is hard to think that Eudoxus was not caught up in such debates.

Late in that dialogue, Socrates introduces the following notion (simplifying *Prt.* 365a3–5):

> *Measure* If the good is pleasure and the bad is pain, and if pleasures and pains can be relatively greater or smaller, and more or less numerous, and of greater or lesser intensity, then we can use the measure of pleasure and pain to arrive at a measure of good and bad.

Socrates and Protagoras have already agreed that some pleasures are bad and some pains are good (*Prt.* 351c3–4), and Socrates is aiming to bring out the inconsistency in the popular combination of thoughts that pleasure is the good and that it is possible to fail to do what one thinks is better because one has been 'overcome by pleasure' (*Prt.* 355d5). As a result, many commentators have been puzzled that anything like *Measure* should have a role in the discussion. Indeed, Clerk Shaw thinks that Socrates 'introduces hedonism without any apparent prompting' (Shaw 2015, p. 1). So the hunt is on for a prompt. For instance, Julia Annas proposes that, with *Measure*, Protagoras is forced into accepting 'a position in argument that he was unwilling to take on' (Annas 1999, p. 170); conversely, Daniel Russell sees Protagoras as being offered 'a friendly aid to his cause' (Russell 2005, p. 248). The tension between these readings is so strong that it is attractive to think that Socrates' talk of measuring and weighing is a matter of 'analogies' or 'metaphors' (Warren 2014, pp. 206–14).

An alternative way to relieve the tension would be to suggest that Plato was prompted to take *Measure* into consideration because it expresses a view arising from discussions of the themes treated in the *Protagoras*. Whether it was Plato who put it into play and thus inspired Eudoxus to take up and perhaps elaborate such a position, or it was Eudoxus who found Speusippus' talk of the indeterminacy of pleasures perplexing, it may be attractive to attribute this textual quirk to 'prompting' external to the text (Davies 2017).

The thrust of *Measure* is that, if pleasure is measurable, and pleasure is the good, then the good is measurable. Earlier in the dialogue it was agreed that pleasure and the good are the same thing (*Prt.* 354c), so that the word 'pleasure' can take the place of the word 'good' (*Prt.* 355c). Socrates' further proposal with *Measure* adds up to a quantitative version of hedonism. The quantities proposed are those of size, number and intensity, although the units to be adopted are not specified, nor how they might be integrated one with another, nor yet how they in turn map onto eventual measures of goodness.

Socrates' first illustration of this thought is to liken the competent reckoner of pleasures to someone who knows how to establish relative weights with the use of scales (*Prt.* 356b1–2; cf. *Euthyph.* 7c). For this sort of operation, no units are necessary: we can just see where the preponderance is. Socrates seems to have in his sights the ways we can fail to use scales aright. What he questions is whether present and future pleasures and pains differ when considered purely as pleasures and pains (*Prt.* 356a8), and he supposes that his interlocutors will think not. If a future pleasure is as pleasant as a present one, then its being in the future should not make any difference to the use of the scales to ascertain its weight and therefore value. The parallelism here is with size and distance: the size of an item is not affected by how far away it is, although distant things will appear to be smaller than nearby things of the same size. But someone who has skill in judging distances will not be deceived, as one who knows the value of certain pleasures will not be 'dragged about like a slave' (352c2) by those that happen to be at hand. Even if the evaluation he arrives at is mistaken, it is still the result of an effort at measuring the pleasures available. The mistake – and the 'enslavement' – arises out of an unjustified preference for what is to hand. A self-controlled hedonist like Eudoxus will thus not be enslaved.

A further complication is introduced at 356b5–6, where it is suggested that both pleasures and pains should be put in the pans of the scales. While Socrates begins with the idea that pleasures can be measured against each other, the addition of pains into the weighing process must mean that what are being weighed are not pleasures but something more like potential courses of action that are associated with certain nets of pleasure and pain. And, of course, it is possible for such associations to go awry and for the nets to be mistakenly assigned to less than optimal courses of action. Perhaps this is reflected in the unobjectionable locution that one 'weighs one's options', and what are being weighed are already results of calculations – rather than weighings – by which pains are subtracted from pleasures. Yet a guide to decision-making need not require that pleasures and pains be measurable on a single scale, with pleasures counting positive and pains negative units.

Socrates then drops the idea of comparing weights and elaborates it, swiftly and rather allusively, with that of discounting irrelevant factors in reckoning quantities at a distance. Here he is picking up at least verbally the first of the factors set out in *Measure*: the 'bigger' or 'greater' (*meizō*) of *Prt.* 356a3 recurs at c5. In this latter passage, he likens the size of a pleasure to the way that an object will look larger if it is close up than if it is far away. Conversely, the moon looks the size of a sixpence, though it is very distant and the coin is in my hand. The example is not Socrates', but it serves our purpose because the text is very cramped. Likewise, the notion of the intensity of a pleasure seems to be modelled by the way that a shout from afar may sound fainter than even a whisper in my ear. Again, the concrete case is supplied, because Socrates does not spell the analogy out, though perhaps he should have. Along with other cues, these optical and acoustic effects enable us to work out how we are placed relative to the things in our environment: if a sixpenny piece subtended the same angle to my eye irrespective of where it was placed relative to me, I would be quite at a loss to know how far away it is from me.

The analogies between the reckoning of the spatial extents of such things as the moon and the sixpence, and the estimates of pleasures and pains, may have a certain intuitive appeal, but, as in the case of the scales, Socrates' gestures at them carry with them some further oddities.

Where, in *Measure*, we have three dimensions of pleasures – size, number and intensity – the spatial analogy can model only one of these – size – and then only by relying on implicit analogies with different sensory modalities. Oddly, Socrates also suggests that numerosity (*ta polla*) will appear to vary with distance (*Prt.* 356c7), perhaps because there are some, relatively rare, cases in which distance does interfere with the count we give of the objects we see: we might see a forest up ahead but not the individual trees. Still, it would be more accommodating to the hedonist view that Socrates is apeing, which we are supposing to have been voiced by Eudoxus, to allow that three coins close up visibly have the same numerosity as three towers in the distance.

Likewise, Socrates' supposed interlocutor is free to say that, where space has three dimensions (up–down, back–forth and left–right), what is at issue in choosing pleasures is always and only the future. Moreover, where the disposition of space seems homogeneous, differing levels of unpredictability in our circumstances may mean that our priorities in choosing pleasures may vary from moment to moment. In times of great uncertainty about our future, such as war, immediate pleasures may reasonably be allowed to be more salient objects of choice than in periods of tranquillity. Even in more tranquil times, we may be in a position to discount the future costs of, for example, a mortgage in order to have the immediate benefit of home ownership because we do care more about now than later.

The 'intuitive appeal' that we have grudgingly allowed to the analogies of the scales and of reckoning quantities in space may come out in light of the contrast that Socrates employs. If one is inept in the use of scales or unable to grasp that the moon is bigger than a sixpence, then one will be subject to the 'power of appearance' (*tou phainomenou dunamis*: *Prt.* 356d4). If one succumbs to the appearances of pleasures that seem big but are not, that seem numerous but are not, and that seem intense but are not, then one will bungle everything and not live a life of pleasure even if that is all one is aiming at. What the use of the scales and the capacity to estimate quantities at a distance are supposed to exemplify is 'the art of measuring' (*hē metrētikē technē*: first at *Prt.* 356d4 and then, in quick succession, at d8, e3 and 4, 7a1, b2 and 4, d7). The art of measuring, then, is a guard against the illusion (*phantasma*, 356d8) imposed by the power of appearance.

At *Protagoras*, 357b6–7, Socrates suddenly says that they will have to put off to another time the enquiry into what the art or science of measuring consists in. Though a *metrētikē technē* recurs, at least verbally, in the *Statesman* (283d1, 284e2, 285a1 and c1 and 286d1), there it is associated with the art of ruling and, in line with the agreement between Socrates and Protagoras at *Prt.* 352c4, concerns knowledge of goods and evils rather than of pleasures and pains.

In short, Plato's handling of what may have been Eudoxus' proposal of a sort of quantitative hedonism as expressed in *Measure* seems rather dismissive. Socrates expounds a caricature version of the doctrine with a view to embarrassing Protagoras' refusal of the unity of the virtues that follows from the identity of virtue with knowledge. Instead of examining the proposed measures of size, number and intensity, Socrates twists these into weight and distance. So it is less than surprising that the upshot is rather inconclusive.

2.2 Propinquity

After it goes off the scene in the *Protagoras*, the sort of quantitative hedonism that Plato formulates in the curious way he does disappears for more than two millennia, at least in the Western philosophical tradition. Nor does it make itself felt in what Aristotle says about Eudoxus' views, which might raise a legitimate doubt about whether Plato had Eudoxus' expressed views in his sights, but rather something he was at best inspired by Eudoxus to think about. Nevertheless, in his *Letter to Menoeceus* (carried by Diogenes, X.130), Epicurus makes a brief mention of the measuring of pleasures against pains, but the idea of calculating hardly figures in the tradition of hedonism that takes more or less direct inspiration from him (Jones 1989; Wilson 2009; Palmer 2014, esp. ch. 2).

But it may be worth taking up a point that we skated over in the last section regarding the relation of quantities of pleasure to time, but that re-emerges in some more recent theorising about the ethical value of pleasure. The point arises from a dialectic that Socrates plays out for Protagoras' benefit in two brief passages adjacent to the enunciation, at *Prt.* 356a3–5, of *Measure*, which we have been associating with something Eudoxus may have said. In these passages, there seem to be in play two other virtual interlocutors who are (even) harder to identify.

The starting point is at *Prt.* 354e6–7, where Socrates begins to interrogate the phrase 'being overcome by pleasure': if pleasure and the good are to be identified, then this would amount to being overcome by the good. But being overcome by pleasure is meant to *explain* doing evil. Then, at *Prt.* 355d6, Socrates imagines himself cross-examining someone, *A*, who is charged with inconsistently holding both the identity of the good and pleasure as well as the possibility of knowing what is better while failing to act on it because he is overcome by pleasure. After the introduction of *Measure*, at *Prt.* 356a6, we seem to have another imagined interlocutor, *B*, who, instead of prioritising differences in size, number and intensity of pleasures, says how great the difference is between immediate pleasures and pleasures-and-pains at a later time, where the former are to be privileged.

What *A* and *B* have in common is that both take the difference between immediate and distant pleasures and pains as making a significant difference to our choices. *A* has been overcome by an immediate pleasure because he sees it as different from future pleasures and pains, which he simply ignores. *B* endorses the priority *A* gives to time. But, if *A* or *B* were in possession of the 'art of measuring', they could preserve the idea that virtue is knowledge by redescribing 'being overcome by pleasure' as a failure of correct measurement.

From what we shall see in the next section about the temperance attributed to Eudoxus, it is unlikely that Plato was ventriloquising him in enunciating the views of *A* and *B*. But a straw poll of educated and generally well-behaved persons, as well as professors of moral philosophy known to the present author, would indicate that a partiality for the temporal proximity of pleasures is quite widespread. 'When do we want it?' 'Now!' It is perhaps, therefore, curious that this partiality does not seem to figure in philosophical discussions of pleasure until near the end of the eighteenth century.

In section II of chapter IV of Jeremy Bentham's *Introduction to the Principles of Morals and Legislation* (2nd ed. 1823), we are told about the 'circumstances' to be taken into account in measuring a lot of pleasure or pain. The fourth of these, after intensity, duration and certainty, is what Bentham calls 'propinquity', which he contrasts with 'remoteness'. Though 'propinquity' has become something of a joke word (e.g. Wodehouse 1943, p. 401), the legal sense that may have brought it to Bentham's attention is closeness of family tie, such as that between father and daughter (Shakespeare *King Lear* I, i, 121). But Bentham seems to be using it to mean immediacy in time.

While propinquity is surely a 'circumstance' of a given pleasure, we have already seen that it is very hard to understand how it can figure in the measurement of it. As with the moon and sixpence, propinquity seems likely to distort our measurement. That a certain lot of pleasure is within our reach should not, of itself, make any difference to whether we choose it or not, especially if a larger lot will make itself available in the long run.

Bentham's inclusion of propinquity as a proper measure has not perhaps become 'official' utilitarian doctrine; Mill, for instance, pays much more attention to the qualities of pleasures (Mill 1861; Donner 1998; West 2004 ch. 3). Yet it is not negligible that, in applications of a 'felicific calculus' that we find in technocratic talk of cost-benefit analysis, for instance concerning the advisability of certain public projects, there is often a marked emphasis on the short-term benefits of some scheme, which is taken to be a factor that speaks in its favour. As already indicated, there is often overlap between what is likely to be within our grasp and what is in the near future; yet these are not measures of value but of prudence, given that the far future is harder to predict, making it harder to be confident about how to evaluate potential pleasures and pains.

2.3 Why Philebus Is Not Given the Time of Day

In virtually all the Platonic dialogues that carry a person's name as their title, the person named is among Socrates' main interlocutors. Not so in the *Philebus*, which recounts a discussion of the role of pleasure in the good life between Socrates and the youthful Protarchus, son of Callias (*Phil.* 19b4; cf. 36d6) and pupil of Gorgias (*Phil.* 58a8–9), who is mentioned by Aristotle as extending the meaning of 'fortunate' (*entychos*) to include also the revered stones of a temple (*Phys.* II.6, 197b10–12). If Protarchus is a pretty solidly historical character, there is room for uncertainty about Philebus. His name is not common and is rather too fitting for a lover of pleasure to be put down to chance. So it may have been some sort of nickname, or, to use a trope that is sometimes useful in handling the characters in Platonic dialogues, a 'mask' (Reale 1997, pp. 16–24).

If the shocking doctrine that pleasure is the good was associated with Eudoxus, and we are allowed to think that he had made his second, longer, visit to the Academy before Plato composed the *Philebus*, which is generally supposed to be among the later dialogues, it is not wild to suppose that Philebus is a mask for Eudoxus. Indeed, some commentators, such as Migliori (2000, pp. 30–1), are quite sure that he is; while others, such as Gosling (1975, pp. 139–41) are sure only that Eudoxus' presence was a spur to the dialogue's composition (cf. Karpp 1933, pp. 23–7; Giannantoni 1958, pp. 145–54; also Gosling and Taylor 1982, pp. 157–64). While doubts have been raised about using the *Philebus* as a source for Eudoxus' hedonism (e.g. Aufderheide 2021, pp. 193–4), the puzzle remains why Plato does not introduce him under his own name. After all, a string of eminent real-life philosophers get drubbed in dialogues named after them; so at least this much seems clear: it is not out of deference for Eudoxus that he is not Plato's direct and explicit target.

In the opening moves of the dialogue, Socrates enunciates the identity of the good with enjoyment, pleasure and delight (*chairein*; *hēdonē*; *terpsis*: *Phil.* 11b4–5), which Philebus recognises as his own view (11c4), but has already renounced any effort to defend it (11a7–8). So it is down to Protarchus to do what he can to defend the view in question. A great deal in the ensuing dialogue has to do with the value to be attributed to pleasure, and there is the fascinating thought, approached from at least three angles (36 c-40e; 41a-2 c and 42 c-44a), that, like beliefs, pleasures can be false: a thought that has generated an enormous literature (see Frede 1992); But it is notable that Protarchus very quickly concedes that the choiceworthy life is one that mixes pleasure with intelligence or practical wisdom (*phronēsis*: 22a3). And the rest of the dialogue proceeds on this premise.

While Eudoxus might have allowed that *phronēsis* is instrumental in attaining pleasure, it is the pleasure that counts, not the means for attaining it. So Protarchus' concession is not entirely loyal to what Philebus or Eudoxus might have said, had they been ready to argue their case. Arguing one's case, especially against the likes of Socrates, is an exercise of reason (*logos*). But Plato may be insinuating the thought that, if the purest form of hedonism is coherent, its defender is forbidden to make use of reason, because to have recourse to reason is to admit, albeit implicitly, that something other than pleasure is of value in life. If anyone is a 'pure' hedonist, Plato will not allow him to argue for what he believes. Conversely, it is useless to argue against the pure hedonist, because he is impervious to reason.

In the coming sections, we shall try to eke out what we can of Eudoxus' arguments for hedonism, and with a view to showing that the reasons in its favour are not negligible.

3 Witness

3.1 Exemplifying Moderation and Advocating Pleasure

The consideration in favour of Eudoxus' hedonism that we look at in this section was not proposed by Eudoxus himself. It was aired, but not wholeheartedly endorsed, by Aristotle in the course of his exposition of arguments in favour of the ethical importance of pleasure in *EN* X. The passage is an aside in the course of that exposition, and runs as follows:

> His words inspired belief more because of the excellence of his [*sc.* Eudoxus'] character than because of themselves; for he was reputed to be a man of exceptional moderation[1] so it was thought that he held his views not as a lover of pleasure but because that is how things really are. (*EN* X.2, 1172b15–8)

Aristotle does not contest the good reputation that Eudoxus enjoyed; he knew him at least as well as anyone in Athens did and would have known it had his reputation been undeserved, had Eudoxus been, after all, a 'lover of pleasure'.

---

[1] In agreement with Aufderheide (2020 *ad loc.*), we suggest this as a rendering of '*sōphrōn*', which in many Aristotelian contexts might be rendered as 'prudence': it is the virtue of proper reaction to bodily pleasures just as courage is the proper reaction to situations of danger. Some translators (Ross (1925); Thomson (1953)) here use 'self-control', which has an air of reining oneself in (as it were against impulse); and others 'temperance' (Rackham 1934), which might bring to mind abstinence from alcohol, but does not quite carry over to the adjective 'temperate' which appears in Barnes' revision of Ross (Barnes 1984), for all that it brings to mind lovely summer's days (Shakespeare, *Sonnet* 18).

But he distances himself from the idea that Eudoxus' good reputation is a strong motive for accepting the arguments he set out for his view that pleasure is the good. Aristotle's stand would be that what really counts is how strong those arguments are, rather than the character of the person proposing them. At a first approximation, then, Aristotle would be deprecating a widespread view that could be set out as an argument like the following:

Witness 1
Eudoxus says that pleasure is the good
What Eudoxus says about the good is credible, given the excellence of his character
(therefore)
It is credible that pleasure is the good

The claim would be that the excellence of Eudoxus' character makes him a credible witness about the nature of the good. If this is what is at stake in *Witness 1*, then Aristotle has every right to be less than convinced. To be a credible witness about the nature of the good, Eudoxus ought to have some sort of advantage or privileged access to knowledge about the matter. But this does not seem to follow from the excellence of his character. After all, it is common experience that persons of good character can nevertheless express themselves unreliably about what guides their attitudes and behaviour. Likewise, Eudoxus' expertise in geometry and astronomy does not seem relevant to his credibility in matters of moral doctrine. In any case, Aristotle was aware that, when he strayed beyond his special competences in mathematics, Eudoxus was at least as unreliable as anyone else, for instance, in his garbled account of the 'mixture' of (quasi-Platonic) Forms with matter (see *Metaph.* I.9, 991a14–9. and XIII.5, 1079b18–23. (= Lasserre D1); cf. Dancy 1991).

If *Witness 1* is not a strong argument, it may nevertheless be instructive to consider how the Athenians might have been struck by a peculiarity in Eudoxus' position, which we might bring out by considering the interrelations among the terms in play:

(i) holding the view that pleasure is the good;
(ii) being a hedonist;
(iii) being moderate; and
(iv) being a lover of pleasure.

Witness 1 presupposes that (iii) makes a case in favour of (i). In turn, (i) appears to imply not only (ii) but also (iv). But, in one way of taking (iv), the lover of pleasure is anything but moderate. Taken in this way, (iii) and (iv) are inconsistent. But there are at least two ways of taking 'lover of pleasure'.

If the Athenians took 'lover of pleasure' to mean someone who indulges in what we might call the pleasures of the flesh, then (iii) and (iv) do indeed present an inconsistency. For, as Aristotle remarks, moderation (*sōphronsunē*) has principally to do with the pleasures that humans share with other animals, such as eating and sex (*EN* III.10, 1118a21-b4). Yet, pleasures of these sorts have usurped the surname (*klēronomos*) 'pleasure' both because we encounter them most often and because everyone is capable of them: because they are the primary sorts that are recognised, it is thought that they are the only sorts there are (*EN* VII.13, 1153b33–5). But they are not the only sort, just as Hoover is not the only brand of vacuum cleaner, though it has given us a verb in a way that Dyson has not.

Because of their familiarity and availability, the pleasures of the flesh have attracted attention to themselves. But there are people, such as Eudoxus, who dedicate themselves to geometry and astronomy. If such activities are not regarded by most people as sources of pleasure, because they are not pleasures of the flesh, then the likes of Eudoxus will not seem to be 'lovers of pleasure', though they do what they do for the pleasure of it. All the same, people who are put off by geometry and astronomy are nevertheless unlikely to be strangers to pleasures that it would be misleading to call 'fleshly'. For instance, making or getting a joke, inventing or solving a riddle, or appreciating a landscape or a fine athletic performance are surely sources of pleasure available to most humans, and many animals indulge in forms of play. Unlike the pleasures of the flesh, these do not tend to excess, so that the lovers of them may indeed be moderate. For such pleasures as these, (iv) is not in conflict with (iii).

So one thing that may have impressed the Athenians was that Eudoxus could take pleasure in activities that were as much beyond their ken as their badinage was beyond their dogs'. In any case, if a person of recognised moderation argues in favour of pleasure as the good, it would be out of place to accuse her of self-extenuation: her character is enough to show that maintaining the doctrine of hedonism does not commit one to a dissolute lifestyle. What's more, if she is a sober and sensible kind of person, we have reason to listen to what she says and, even if we remain unconvinced, we do not reject what she says on the grounds of her character.

3.2 Impartial Judges

One thing that humans, dogs and many other animals share is what Aristotle calls the perceptual soul, one that is responsive to the environment by way of the senses. This responsiveness in turn is a capacity for pleasure and pain (*De An.*,

II, ii, 413b23–4; iii, 414b3–5; III, vii, 431a9–12; xi, 434a3), and the pleasures in question seem to be identifiable as the sort we have been calling 'fleshly'. Even if possession of a perceptual soul is necessary for the enjoyment of fleshly pleasures, if there are pleasures that are not fleshly, then these may be enjoyed by beings that do not have a sensitive soul.

According to a certain tradition in Christian thought, angels do not have a perceptual soul (Thomas *ST*, I, 51 and 54); therefore, they do not enjoy fleshy pleasures. So, if Eudoxus had proposed his doctrine on the nature of the good to a Thomistic angel, the angel would not have rejected it on the grounds that push severe (human) moralists to do so, namely because of its association with servile and bestial pleasures. We might even imagine an angel accepting the identity of its pleasure in contemplating the divine with the good. But, even so, we might think that this was a sort of partiality no less than that of a human who identified the pleasures of the fleshly desire satisfaction with the good. For the angel would be ignorant of a sort of pleasure that humans are acquainted with.

In light of what we have already seen about how the pleasures that humans share with other animals have usurped the 'surname' of pleasure, we might imagine a language in which there were separate words for those pleasures that require a perceptual soul ('*woohoo*') and those, like those of an angel, that do not ('*ahah*'), but in which there was no word for the genus of which *woohoo* and *ahah* are supposed, by usage in at least a few other languages, to be species. The speakers of such a language would not suppose that the *woohoo* exhaust some class of which the *ahah* are fully paid-up members. Of course, there might be cases in which it is unclear whether we have to do with *woohoo* or *ahah*, just as English speakers may be unsure in some cases whether they have to do with bliss, delight, satisfaction, gratification or fun, each of which seems to be a species of which pleasure may be thought the genus.[2] Yet, unlike English, in which 'the good is pleasure' naturally enough encompasses also these species, in this supposed language, Eudoxus' hedonist thesis would have to be expressed by saying, 'the good is *woohoo* and *ahah*'.

Our supposed language would remove the surprise that a hedonist like Eudoxus is not a slave to the attractions of *woohoo*, because he cultivates *ahah*. But it would not be profitable to try to reform English to separate by neologism the senses of 'pleasure' that *woohoo* and *ahah* mark. After all, we can

---

[2] I would be intrigued to hear of a language in which no single word ranged over the phenomena over which range words like '*hēdonē*', 'voluptas', 'pleasure', 'plaisir', 'placer', 'Lust', 'nöje', 'piacere', 'plezuro', 'pryzymność' or '*naslazhdenie*'. My impression is that, in at least some of these languages, genus–species distinctions analogous to those cited for English can be made out; for Prodicus' effort to make them out for Greek, see Wolfsdorf 2011, and Bett 2020 §4. Given that I have recently had notice of a language (Kusunda, in western Nepal, with only one fluent native speaker) that has no word for 'no', I am open to surprises.

already – when we remember to – operate a distinction between fleshly pleasures and the others that do not depend essentially on the perceptual soul. Moreover, we might be induced into the error opposite to the one that Aristotle draws attention to with his remark about the 'surname' and forget the close connection – if only because of what motivates us – between *woohoo* and *ahah* that makes them both kinds of pleasure.

3.3 The Moderation of Eudoxus: An Example to Us All

The moderation that Aristotle reports being attributed to Eudoxus is a state of character of one who acts willingly: 'he abstains from fleshly pleasure and finds this abstinence itself pleasurable' (*EN* II.3, 1104b5–6). Like many virtues, moderation falls between two opposites. In one direction, there is intemperance (*akolasia*), which is the tendency to give in to servile and bestial pleasures, while the other extreme, called *anaisthesia* (*EN* II.7, 1107b6ff.), is so rare as hardly to count as a vice, but more like the clinical conditions that we nowadays call anorexia or anhedonia.

Given that the pleasures that give rise to intemperance are also connected with the survival of individual animals (food) and of the species (sex), it is hardly surprising that they have a deep and lasting hold on us. If only for this reason, the virtue of *sōphrosunē* is a rare thing: it has to manage – when it is not in direct conflict with – drives that have a strong biological base. To counteract these drives, which tend to excess, most people have to – and generally do – exercise self-control (*enkrateia*). But, because this is something of an effort for most people, we are subject to episodes of incontinence (*akrasia*), which is sometimes rendered as 'weakness of the will'. Yet, in the exercise of self-control, especially with a view to acquiring the virtue of moderation, a person may deny themselves a pleasure to which they are, so to say, entitled.

To capture the difference between the moderation attributed to Eudoxus and what we have been calling self-control, we may recall this observation:

> When pleasure is on trial, we are not impartial judges. The line to take is that of treating it as the [Trojan] elders treated Helen and to repeat what they said; for if we keep it at a distance, we are less likely to go astray. (*EN* II.9, 1109b8–12)

The point that Aristotle is aiming to make with this Homeric allusion (*Iliad* 3.156–60) is that, as the beauty of Helen made men lose their heads, so the attraction we feel for pleasures – especially fleshly pleasures – makes us unreliable in evaluating them impartially. Not putting ourselves in temptation's way helps us exercise self-control, and our judgement is not clouded by the terror or vertigo that afflicts someone who recognises, and perhaps overestimates, the dangers of excess.

A similar point may emerge from the following analogies. While Kant notoriously says that from the crooked timber of humanity nothing perfectly straight can be made (1784, §6), Aristotle suggests that we can correct our vicious tendencies by erring in the opposite direction, 'as people do in straightening sticks that are bent' (*EN* II.9, 1109b6–7). Likewise, in an adjacent passage of *EN* Aristotle alludes to the episode in which Odysseus ties himself to his ship's mast so that he can hear but not be brought to ruin by the sirens (*Odyssey* 12.204–13), while it is said that Kant had his arms tied by his side as he slept so that he could not play with himself (see Botul 1999, 5).

The claim in Eudoxus' favour would then be that he can look straight at Helen and appreciate her beauty, and can listen to and enjoy the sirens' song without going overboard. Because he has straightened himself out, he need not be deflected one way or the other. If this claim were what the Athenians believed, then we would have a slightly different argument from *Witness 1* about his authority in matters of morals:

Witness 2
Eudoxus says that pleasure is the good
What Eudoxus says about pleasure is credible, given the excellence of his character
(therefore)
It is credible that pleasure is the good

Given that this emerges from Aristotle's own distinction between moderation and self-control, he might have been less cautious in following the Athenians' admiration of Eudoxus.

4 Addition

4.1 Pleasure a Good Added to Good Action

In the swift rundown of Eudoxus' arguments for hedonism in *EN* X.2, the last in the list is also the weakest both in the sense of making the least bold claim and in the sense of being most exposed to obvious objections. Aristotle's report of it runs as follows:

> The addition of pleasure to a good, such as being just or moderate, makes it more choiceworthy (*hairetōteron*), and only the good can increase something of the same sort. (*EN* X.2 1172b23–6)

As presented in connection with Eudoxus, *Addition* does not exclude (a) that there are goods other than pleasure, which, as had already been argued in the *Philebus* (60b-e), proves that pleasure is not *the* good; (b) that there are goods that are more choiceworthy than pleasure; (c) that there are pleasures that are not goods; nor (d) that there are pleasures that are evils when they are added to evils.

It should emerge in the coming sections that the argument we call *Honour* responds in some measure to (a); *End* to (b); and *Opposites* to (c). For the present, we concentrate on (d), first trying to see what an argument like Eudoxus' *Addition* argument is getting at; then examining a near-fatal objection to hedonism that arises against it; and, finally, suggesting an understanding of choiceworthiness that to some degree defuses the objection.

A swift way to get to the nub of *Addition* is to consider that the justice and moderation invoked in Aristotle's report of the argument are virtues. To act in line with these virtues is to aim, respectively, at certain distributions of goods and at a certain level of consumption for oneself. If one pursues these aims under what we might call external pressure, for instance to earn a good name or avoid reproof, then one acts out of what we have already heard Aristotle call '*enkrateia*', which need not involve going with the flow of one's immediate inclinations. But, if one does what is just or moderate freely and wholeheartedly – because it feels like the thing to do – then so doing will be a source of pleasure. Even a person who has not entirely internalised justice or moderation and, so, may be said to be enkratic, may on occasion – or even fairly frequently, if the person is well advanced in the internalisation of the virtue – act spontaneously in line with the virtue in question. In such cases, there will be one good, which is that of, say, giving to each according to his deserts; and there will be another, which is that of seeing justice done. Especially when the judge has nothing to gain from the distribution at issue, this latter is a pleasure available primarily to persons who have internalised the virtue of justice. And *mutatis mutandis* for the moderation that was associated with Eudoxus: eating the right amount of the right food satisfies appetite as well as restoring one to vigour.

In the form that Aristotle attributes to Eudoxus, the basic thrust of *Addition* appears to depend on the idea that adding pleasure to the performance of an action increases the value of that action.

4.2 Pleasure in Corrupt Behaviour

While the basic thrust of *Addition* seems to work well enough when applied to actions performed in conformity with virtue, it is easy to see that it cannot be generalised.

Taking up a suggestion in Moore's *Principia Ethica* (1903, §125), we may imagine two worlds that are otherwise identical. In one of them, a (let us suppose, innocent) person is being tortured and a spectator is pained by what is going on; in the other, the spectator is enjoying the scene. Since the latter is the world in which there is more pleasure and less suffering than in the former, it should be the one that the hedonist prefers. But this seems quite wrong. If we were ourselves in the position of the spectator, it would be better if we were upset by what we see than to participate in the pleasure of the sadist who is inflicting the torture.

A dogmatic or desperate hedonist might respond to a case like this by saying that we need to be educated to do our calculations more exactly: even sadistic pleasures are pleasures, which explains why sadists cultivate them. But this is just the kind of line that gets hedonism a bad name as a cover for all sorts of wicked behaviour.

More concessively, it might be allowed that the comparison of the two worlds does indeed produce an embarrassing result for one who aims to maximise pleasure, but the case needs a bit of hedging. For instance, the hedonist might say that the sadist's and his accomplice's pleasures must be counted as less significant than the pain inflicted on the innocent victim. But we might wonder where such a 'must' might come from; has anyone ever carried out such a calculation? And if 'less significant' means 'less in quantity', are we not lacking a reason to think that there is a single scale on which the pleasures and pains involved can be commensurated? Or some utilitarians might say that sadistic pleasures are ill-adapted in the long run to promote the greatest happiness of the greatest number. But privileging the disposition or the rule over the episode might generate a further doubt: isn't the *locus* of pleasure ultimately in how the subject responds to the given situation?

4.3 Merely Apparent Pleasure

If Eudoxus is to furnish a more robust response to a Moorean challenge to *Addition*, he might appeal to the idea that, appearances to the contrary, the sadist and his accomplice are not deriving pleasure from torturing their victim.

Such an appeal is risky on at least two counts. In the first place, it makes it almost impossible to explain why the sadist is doing what he is doing if not for the pleasure of it. And, second, it looks like arrogance on the part of Eudoxus to claim to know what pleasure really is, while the sexual pervert does not.

In an effort to rise to this double challenge, we may recur to what was suggested in the previous section about the relation between genuine moderation and the pleasure that the moderate person takes in pleasures that are not bestial and servile. In a sense indicated in the second premise of *Witness 2*, the moderate person is one who knows about pleasure. Indeed, Aristotle goes further and proposes that the virtuous and good person is the measure (*metron*) of what is genuinely pleasurable (*EN* X.5 1176a18–20).

This sort of move is of a piece with how Aristotle connects true or focal instantiations of virtues with their counterpart or degenerate cases. For instance, the warrior who willingly and knowingly confronts the dangers of battle is genuinely courageous, while one who does his duty out of fear of humiliation is courageous only in an imperfect sense (*EN* III.6–8). Likewise, Aristotle supposes that genuine friendship is a relation of reciprocal benevolence between virtuous adult males (*EN* VIII.13–14; also *EE* VII.2, presumably derived from Plato, *Lysis*, 299 c-d), yet he might at a stretch – or in some sort of metaphorical sense – allow that there can be friendship between humans and animals ('a dog is a man's best friend'). The notions of courage and friendship are already value-laden, whether or not we share Aristotle's own values, for example, about courage as an essentially military virtue or about the demotion of women in relation to friendship (but see Connell 2021, pp. 41–4). Yet it is not a surprise to find a similar formal structure applied to moderation and, so, to pleasures.

To respond, then, to the sadist's taking pleasure in torturing or the spectator's pleasure in witnessing the scene, we are on the look out for a model on which their pleasures stand to Eudoxus' as cowardice and selfishness stand to courage and friendship respectively. If such a model can be made plausible, then it is not an arbitrary matter that Eudoxus' pleasures are the genuine ones, and the charge of arrogance is at least blunted.

In his discussions of depraved pleasures both in VII.5 and in X.3 of *EN* Aristotle makes more explicit use of medical terminology than we find in his accounts of excess and defect relative to other virtues. Indeed, at *EN* X.3 1173a24, he asks rhetorically why we cannot say that pleasure is like health, which he takes to be the natural state of the organism. But with our sadist and others, we have to deal with cases where something is awry. Such morbid states may be brought on by external causes, as Aristotle supposes in some cases of pederasty, which may be the result of childhood abuse (*EN* VII.5 1148b30–1), while others are due to poor upbringing (1148b17–9). But such things will appear pleasant to the subject, just as unwholesome food may taste good to someone who is ill (*EN* X.3 1173b23). On these sorts of grounds, Aristotle goes so far as to deny that such apparent pleasures are even pleasant (1173b20).

If the cost of this last move is to downplay the subjective aspect of the experience of pleasure, then we might do well to look more closely at the relationship that seems to be presupposed in *Addition* between acting well – justly or moderately – and the pleasure that accrues to it.

4.4 Flows and Energy

In Section 3.2, we imagined a language in which two varieties of pleasure are separated in the language's basic vocabulary, as between those that require a perceptual soul of the sort Aristotle refers to (*woohoo*) and those adapted to beings, such as Thomistic angels, that do not have a perceptual soul (*ahah*). The native speakers of such a language might be oblivious to such relations as do obtain between these varieties. Though the hypothesis of such a language was by way of parody, it is noticeable how, down the millennia, from the Epicurean distinction between 'kinetic' and 'katastematic' pleasures (frs. 127–9 and 416 Usener, on implications of which see Nikolsky 2001) to Gilbert Ryle's discrimination of desire-satisfactions from enjoyments (Ryle 1954, IV), dichotomies not so far removed from that imagined between *woohoo* and *ahah* have been prominent in theorising about the roles that pleasure might play in moulding action. It is also worth recalling in this connection the sorts of genus–species relations that we referred to in Section 3.3.

Here we arrive at something of a crossroads. In one direction, and in line with what we gestured at referring (in Section 3.1) to the pleasures of joking and such, we might be looking for some sort of continuum among various sorts of pleasure that does not lend itself to the sharp – albeit not altogether convincing – disjunctions that have been proposed. Along the other road, there is something attractive in saying that the pleasures of eating and sex are, after all, different in kind from those, such as the mathematical exercises Eudoxus privileged, that have a strongly intellectual component.[3] And it looks as if we can take no more than one of these roads, on pain of talking 'sheer babble' (Anscombe 1958, p. 27).

But there may be a third route through this thicket. On what we have already alluded to as a subjectivist or psychological model of pleasures, a pleasure is taken to be in some way a sensation or a characteristic of some sensations. Thus, the pleasure of a given sort – whether it is that of seeing someone being tortured, eating a wholesome meal or demonstrating a geometrical theorem – would be an affect that accompanies the activity and is brought about by it. In Aristotelian terms, it would count as a movement or a becoming (*kinesis*). But one point that Aristotle concedes to Speusippus regarding pleasure is that 'no becoming belongs to the same genus as its end' (*EN* VII.11, 1152b12–5). The example he repeatedly uses for illustrating this sort of distinction (or, more likely, family of interrelated distinctions), which can be boiled down to that between a potentiality (*dunamis*) and an actuality (*energeia*), is that of the relation between the process of building a house and the completed house (*EN* VII

---

[3] Indeed, Cicero (*Tusc.* III.18; *Fin.* II.9–16) goes so far as to accuse the Epicureans of a sort of equivocation in using the same word for the pleasures of the body and those of the soul.

11,, also *Metaph.*, IX.6 and *Phys.* III.1). But Aristotle observes – against Speusippus' strictures on pleasure as a good – that the enjoyment of a given activity is not incomplete while the activity is under way, in the way that the building of the house is incomplete until the house is finally built.

Rather than think of a pleasure as a process that has some end outside itself, Aristotle likens it to seeing. While I am seeing something, my state with regard to it – my 'seeing' – is complete (*teleia*, *EN* X.4, 1174a14–9); there is nothing to be added to it and prolonging it does not make it more complete. On this analogy, a pleasure is not a movement, but rather the perfection of an activity (*energeia*). To reinforce this analogy and clarify the conceptual point being made, Aristotle adduces two pretty decisive considerations. One is that, if pleasure were a movement or a becoming, then it would make sense to say that a pleasure was fast or slow; but this is evidently not the case (*EN* X.3, 1173a31-b4). The other, specifically aimed at the idea that, among *kinēseis*, if pleasure were a sensation, then it ought to be a distraction from the activity that it accompanies. But precisely the opposite seems to hold: the more pleasure we get from a given activity, the more we are involved in or concentrated on it (*EN* X.5, 1175a31–6 and b7–15). In the hippyish idiom of *Zen and the Art* (Pirsig 1974), it is a matter of 'going with the flow' of an engrossing activity, even that of fixing a motorbike.

These sorts of considerations may help us to understand the respect in which pleasure perfects an activity to which it is appropriate. As well as being a sort of end accompanying (*epiginomenēn*: *EN* II.3 1104b4–5) virtuous actions, it is a perfection that is supervenient (*epiginomenon*: *EN* X.4 1174b34) on them. Though the phrase in which this latter notion appears, invoking 'the bloom of health in vigorous youth', is the direct object of Miss Anscombe's scorn, as cited above, it is perhaps not so hard to understand after all. In one direction, the figure of the 'flower of youth' was perhaps already a dead or dying metaphor when Homer used it in the *Iliad* (XIII.455). In another, the association of genuine beauty with the fit and healthy appears in the *Gorgias* (462c3-d10) and in other Socratic texts, including Xenophon (see Warren 2015), as well as being used by Aristotle himself as an analogy to illustrate the relation between a paralogism and a refutation in good order (*Soph. El.,* 1, 164a26-b21): cosmetics and sophisms are not ultimately convincing though they may beguile for a moment.

The moral that might be drawn is that, if we catch the drift of *Addition*, we do well to think of pleasure in virtuous behaviour not so much as a sort of sweetness but rather as a symptom of a healthy constitution. The relation between an activity and the pleasure that goes with it is not so much one of cause-and-effect as of one in which the pleasure is a collateral accompaniment of what it is to do the right thing.

We still have to respond to the problem of the sadist (and his accomplice). Here we have to avail ourselves of a premise that the sadist would reject, namely, that the infliction of pain on others or the spectacle of others' pain does not carry with it a pleasure that is appropriate to it. For a genuine pleasure must be appropriate to an activity that has an end that is a good; but pain is not a good, as even Speusippus concedes. Hence, causing pain or witnessing its infliction does not have a good as its end.

If there is no pleasure that is appropriate to the infliction or the witnessing of pain, there is nothing that is superadded to the activity of the sadist or the experience of the witness. This does not exclude the possibility that the sadist and his accomplice *believe* that they are taking pleasure in the torture inflicted, nor that that belief is their motivation for bringing about occasions for their apparent pleasures. But the point of *Addition* would be that the belief in question is false because the activity is not choiceworthy (*hairetōteron*, already cited from *EN* X.2 1172b25). As we have conceded, this response need not convince the sadist; but it does at least exonerate the hedonist from having to prefer a world in which sadistic spectacles add to the sum of pleasures.

Even if pleasure is a good-maker of any good (see Aufderheide 2020, pp. 68–71), an argument like *Addition* is consistent with there being good-making characteristics of activities that do not, at least directly, have to do with pleasure. Moreover it is not easy in advance to tell which pleasures are genuinely so, because supervenient on good activities, from those that are deceptive, such as those derived from cruelty. Even if we buy into Aristotle's objectivising tendency in individuating which pleasures are genuine, *Addition* will not deliver a strong version of the hedonism that Eudoxus wants to propose.

5 Honour

5.1 Hierarchising Goods

In our listing, in Section 1.3, of the arguments that Aristotle associates with Eudoxus in favour of identifying pleasure with the good, a preponderance appear in the tenth book of *EN*, especially in chapters 2 and 4. Three of these – *Cradle*, *Witness* and *Opposites* – also break the surface elsewhere in the work and, as we have seen with *Addition*, the reconstruction of the arguments calls for reference to other places not only in the *Ethics* but also in other Aristotelian writings.[4] But the one that we call '*Honour*' is relayed, along with

---

[4] In general, we try to bear in mind Jonathan Barnes' admonition that many Anglophone philosophers 'osent lire l'*Ethique à Nicomaque* (. . .) sans se familiariser avec la *Métaphysique* ou le traité *De l'âme*' (Barnes 1980, p. 706), where the daring verges on the reckless.

the only other reference to Eudoxus by name only in *EN* I.12 (1101b27), though a distinction on which it turns is elaborated in the *Rhetoric* (I.9).

Once more, the question arises, but cannot be settled, of whether Aristotle was consulting some text by Eudoxus or merely recalling informal discussion, either with the man himself or with someone who had heard him talking about the matter in hand. For, the first word of the sentence that interests us is '*dokei*': 'it seems' (*EN* I.12 1101b27); and it may be that the scope of the seeming is whether Eudoxus argued in the way he seems to have argued or whether, in arguing in this way, he seems to have argued well:

> It seems that Eudoxus argued well in favour of the primacy to be accorded to pleasure, for he contended that the fact that, though it is a good, it is not praised (*mē epaineisthai*) points to its being superior to what is praised (*tōn epainetōn*), as god and the good are, because they are what other things are referred to. (*EN* I.12, 1101b27–32)

The brief chapter in which this passage appears is dedicated to the question of whether happiness is one of the things that we praise or rather one of those that we honour (1101b10–2). Though Aristotle exemplifies this distinction between '*epaineō*' on the one hand and '*makarizō*' and '*timaō*' on the other, in terms of appropriate attitudes to courageous men and to gods respectively, we dare to offer some rather homlier contrasts, appealing in the first instance to jargon in use for academic titles.

On the one hand, we have degrees that are awarded on the basis of course work and examination performance. When a candidate has shown excellence in such tasks, the examining board has the option to signal special approval by adjoining to its grading as first class some indicator of outstanding performance, such as a Latinism including some grade of '*cum laude*', as in many American universities. In such cases, we have to do with praise (*epainesis*). On the other hand, universities have the right to confer degrees on persons who have not followed courses or taken exams but who, for one reason or another, have gained the favour of the academic senate or similar body. Often enough, these degrees carry the title 'Doctor' and sometimes they are awarded to eminent scholars who may already be in possession of a PhD because, at an earlier stage in their career, they wrote a dissertation based on their research to earn that title. But sometimes, such titles are awarded to persons who have made some signal impact, either within or outside the realm of academe, for instance in advancing humanitarian causes, playing football rather well or simply donating money to the awarding institution. In such cases, the degree is said to be 'honorary' (*ad honorem* or *honoris causa*) and is taken to signal the glory (*makariotēs, timē*) of the person so honoured.

We may elaborate this binary distinction with reference to the fact that, in order to praise something, we must appeal to some characteristic of higher value. If we have a hierarchy of categories, the members of the highest class cannot be praised, but only honoured or glorified.

For instance, with just three categories, such as 'child', 'adult' and 'god', we can make out some formal characteristics of praising and honouring. It is no praise to say that a child is being childish; when it is not reproof, it may be extenuation. Thus, the praise-relation is irreflexive. It is faint praise to say that an adult is acting like an adult, though one might think that not a few grown-ups are not fully adult in their behaviour, and it is a criticism to describe the behaviour of someone over eighteen or twenty-one as childish. Praising is thus asymmetrical. It is strong praise of a child to say that she is acting like an adult, and if a child, such as Mozart, does something, such as playing a musical instrument, divinely, he is doing so better than might be expected even of the best adult practitioners of the art. This sort of case indicates that praising is transitive. But, from the irreflexivity, it also follows that, in our minischeme of values, one cannot praise a god for doing something divinely, a point that Aristotle makes a few lines above the passage in which he discusses Eudoxus' views (*EN* I.12 1101b20), describing such praise as 'laughable'. For this reason, the BBC religious programme and the hymn book that share the title '*Songs of Praise*' are conceptual muddles (if not outright heretical), while the first line of Gerard Manley Hopkins' 'Pied Beauty': 'Glory be to God for dappled things' gets it spot on.

If the thrust of Eudoxus' *Honour* argument draws on the distinction between praising and honouring, and on the sort of hierarchy we have gestured at, we may look a little more closely at how it applies specifically to pleasure, and at just how strong a conclusion it supports.

5.2 No Way to Praise Pleasure

Taking a further modernising liberty with the conceptual machinery Eudoxus seems to be relying on in *Honour*, we might consider some ways in which attempts to praise pleasure are blocked by considering how an advertising campaign in its favour would run into trouble.

To promote a product, an advert has to refer to characteristics that make it desirable. For instance, to boost a detergent, one has to say that it washes better (or at least no worse) than others or that it comes at a reasonable price, or both. A clean shirt is the end to which washing is the means, and not spending money uselessly is a maxim of good shopping. Because claims to such virtues are hardly more plausible for one brand than for another, much advertising of this sort does little more than keep the names before the public's mind.

In addition to purely commercial advertising, there is a sort of public service broadcasting that seeks to raise awareness about social or ethical problems. Like adverts for detergents, such communications tend to preach to the converted, when they do not run into performative paradox, as when a television announcement advises the public to do something more interesting than watching the television.

What sort of slogan could an advertising campaign in favour of pleasure adopt?

Suppose some bright spark came up with the apparent tautology: 'Choose pleasure: it'll give you pleasure.' On the one hand, this may not even be true: trying to enjoy oneself is one of the finest recipes for not enjoying oneself. On the other, there is the question of who needs to be convinced. Most people much of the time choose to do what they think will, in the long or short term, bring them such satisfactions as are available to them in the circumstances in which they find themselves. Even fools who write (or read) books about the hedonism of Eudoxus of Cnidus presumably do so because most of the alternatives seem grimmer still.

It may be the case that enjoying yourself is good for you. In particular, it has been found that physical exercise tends to reduce depression and anxiety by triggering the release of endorphins (Kolata 2008). But a person to whom such a prescription is made might think it insulting to be told to abandon the comfortable couch on which he is slouching and expose himself as a jogger. Moreover, there are those who think that pleasure is somehow indifferent, and others who even think that pain – even one's own – is a good. To sell pleasure to them requires a rather more elaborate approach than our first slogan can encompass.

In the former case, we might be able to point out to someone who denies that pleasure is naturally preferred to pain that he sits himself comfortably before listening to Eudoxus' battery of arguments in favour of hedonism. If, in the course of the exposition, he so much (or little) as shifts from one buttock to the other, he refutes his own theory that pleasure and pain are not proper prompts to action. In the nature of the case, it is hard to think of anyone who actually holds such a view, except for the sake of argument. And even those, such as the Stoics who held that pleasures and pains are indifferent (*adiaphora*: e.g. Zeno, *SVF* 1.195; Chrysippus, *SVF* 2.155, 181), nevertheless conceded that the former are preferred to the latter (Chrysippus, *SVF* 2.127, 139).[5]

---

[5]　I am grateful to James Warren for getting me to think twice about the various positions in play here.

In the latter, it is often enough the case that the proponent of the positive value of suffering in this life has her eye on a superhedonism of Salvation in a hereafter. If she wants to gamble that way, she is at least not alone (Pascal 1962, 418). The odds in such a wager are rather more imponderable than they are sometimes presented as being (Hacking 1975, ch. 8), but the point remains that, to recommend a present sacrifice, she has to hold out a promise of the reward of eternal beatitude. Which may be nothing but pleasure with brass knobs on, because infinite in intensity and in duration (but perhaps a bit boring[6]).

If our first 'tautological' suggestion about how to recommend pleasure looks vulnerable, at least two other salient options likewise run into problems.

One, which we might think of as 'conflictual', might arise when an adult sees a child sulking at a birthday party, and admonishes: 'whether you like it or not, you are here to have fun.' There may be an element of encouraging the child to relax and be more sociable, but it is not clear that the encouragement will succeed. Though the child may really not be interested in the games being played, it may also be that, if he got into them, he would get carried away. There are innumerable variants on this sort of conflict, from the case of Leontius, whose fascinated revulsion at the corpses piled up outside the walls of Athens is relayed by Plato (*Resp.* IV 439e–440a), through Sidgwick's scruples about publicising his Utilitarianism (Sidgwick 1907, pp. 489–90) down to what Slavoj Žižek calls 'the vagaries of the superego' (Žižek 2021). It goes beyond our present remit to investigate the ways that conflicts of this sort nudge those who are sensitive to them into proposing subdivisions of the soul. But the fact remains that some sort of spontaneity of response is central to the enjoyment of pleasures.

A third sort of slogan we might imagine in favour of cultivating pleasure has a minatory air about it: 'do your duty: be entertained', where the addressee is being coaxed into consuming the products of the industries of 'free time': entertainment, sport, tourism and so on. As Ermanno Bencivenga has astutely noted (Bencivenga 1995), many of these activities have the same structures of automatic repetition that characterise the world of work in capitalistic economies. In one case he considers, that of juvenile soccer in contemporary America (chapter IV), the frenzy with which the game is played means that it loses all contact with the sorts of skill and coordination that characterise sports properly so-called and, so, is evacuated of all source of (aesthetic?) satisfaction. It might be commonplace to call such societies 'hedonistic'; but, insofar as they seem destined to generate frustration and alienation, this might seem a misnomer.

---

[6] Most readers of Dante find *Inferno* much more interesting than *Paradiso*.

There may be ways of avoiding tautology, conflict or threat in promoting pleasure, but it was shrewd of Eudoxus to see that trying to praise it is likely to end us up in tangles.

5.3 On Not Choosing the Life of Pleasure

Drawing on a tradition going back to Pythagoras (made explicit by Iamblichus in his *Introduction to Arithmetic* XII (58)), Aristotle reports a threefold distinction among the sorts of life one might choose to pursue (*EN* I.5): that of pleasure; that of honour and political activity; and that of contemplation. He appears to be endorsing his source when he associates the first of these with the sort of enjoyment (*agapē*, *EN* I.5, 1095b17) that, in the Greek of the time (unlike later Christian usage), meant social eating and drinking, and he immediately dismisses it as slavish and fit only for cattle. While Aristotle concedes that it is difficult for those who are rich and powerful to be also good (*Pol.* IV.11 1259b), the fact that kings such as the Assyrian Sardanapallus (*EN* I.5 1095b22) or the Sybarite Smindiridis (*EE* I.5 1216a16–7) indulged their senses induces people to think that, if those who are free to choose their lifestyle go for such pleasures, that speaks in their favour.

One curious thing about Aristotle's dismissal of this option is that the sorts of pleasures involved are those that we have been tagging 'woohoo'. As already indicated (Sections 3.1 and 3.2), Aristotle himself was well aware of the verbal usurpation here. So there is nothing to stop a passionate astronomer and mathematician like Eudoxus from saying that the life of pleasure that he wishes to cultivate is one prevalently of '*ahah*', which is not in the least bovine.

The life that Eudoxus chooses is given over to contemplation, for instance of matters astronomical and mathematical, which Aristotle recommends in *EN* X 7–8 precisely on the grounds of the high quality and quantity of pleasure it gives, as we shall see in a little more in detail in Section 7.4. But, given that it is laughable to praise the divine, and the pleasure of contemplation has something of the divine about it, it cannot be praised, but is rather to be honoured. This, of course, does not show that the pleasure Eudoxus recommends is unique in the class of things that cannot be praised, but it does indicate that it is at least among the highest goods.

6 Opposites

6.1 Avoiding Pain

Of Eudoxus' battery of arguments in favour of his hedonism, the only one treated in both of Aristotle's discussions of pleasure in books VII and X of the *Nicomachean Ethics* is the one that we have tagged 'Opposites'. It is also the one that Aristotle seems to endorse most wholeheartedly, at least in that he rejects the only objection raised against it. The key passages are as follows:

> It is also generally agreed that pain is an evil and to be avoided; for all pain is either simply evil or an evil in being an impediment. But what is opposite to something that is to be avoided, and opposed to it as a thing to be avoided and, so, an evil, is good. It follows of necessity that pleasure is good. (*EN* VII.13 1153b1–4)

and

> He (*sc.* Eudoxus) maintained that the goodness of pleasure was no less obvious from its opposite, for pain in itself is to be avoided by everybody, so that correspondngly its opposite is to be chosen. (*EN* X.2 1172b18–20)

Despite the verbal variants, we take these passages to be presenting much the same argument.[7] Perhaps it should be made clear from the outset that the sort of opposition that Eudoxus and Aristotle have in mind is what we might call 'axiological' – to do with values.

The value-judgement that it takes as a premise is the badness of pain (cf. *Top.* III.6 119a38-b1). This premise is taken to be more obvious than the conclusion that Eudoxus is aiming at and thus indicates what we might call the direction of proof. One might deny that pain is always and in any case an evil, for instance, when it is a means to some greater pleasure or to avoid greater pain (physical exercise, surgery). Yet it seems that no one in their right mind thinks that pleasure is an evil or that pain is a good as such. As Aristotle says, 'if pleasure were an evil, it would be to be avoided' (*EN* X.2 1173a10); but the intemperate have to take precautions against the attractions of excessive pleasures of the body (especially of the kind we have dubbed *woohoo*) and, as we shall see in the next section, only fanatics like Speusippus propose that pleasure is an evil.

Given that such fanatics are likely to think that pleasure and pain are opposed features of a single physiological system, it may be worth recording not only that bodily pains are generated in at least three distinct nervous systems, but also that an evolutionary-Kiplingesque 'Just-So' story would indicate that, at least as biological evolution on Earth is currently schematised, there was a very long period in which animals suffered pain but none enjoyed pleasure.

---

[7] But see Gosling and Taylor 1982, pp. 225–40, for detailed comparison; Wei Cheng (2020, §3) presents a useful table illustrating how VII aims to show that pleasure is *a* good, while X aims at the stronger conclusion that pleasure is *the* good. As Warren (2009, pp. 251–2) puts it, while VII presents a 'defensive' account of pleasure, X 'explains the positive connection between pleasure and our nature'; likewise, Harte attributes to VII a 'negative ambition' (2014, p. 293), while X concentrates on a causal connection between perfect activity and the pleasure arising from it (pp. 311–4).

Without entering into details, the slowest pain system, which is sensitive to heat and to chemical irritants, transmits information to the brain along the 'C-fibres', so beloved of philosophers, at a velocity of about 0.25 metres per second (nearly eight seconds from my toes to my head); a parallel system, which is between twice and four times as fast, carries messages about the nature of the damage; and the 'A-delta' nerves, which are insulated by myelin (like an electrical wire), signal peripheral damage at up to 120 metres per second. These three sources of information are gated before entering the brain and pass along at least five different cerebral pathways before arriving at the *substantia gelatinosa*. The interruption of these pathways does not prevent the subject from having pleasure, nor does the surgical removal of prefrontal lobes, which is efficacious in relieving otherwise untreatable central pain. Though we have already adverted to some of the various phenomena that are pleasures, their subdivisions do not coincide with the various ways that bodily pain arises.

According to our 'Just-So' story, based what seems to be a scientific consensus, before about 150 million years ago, no organism on the planet was sufficiently complex to suffer pain, which, after all, makes little or no difference to survival or to the transmission of genes: reflexes are quite enough. With the emergence of animals in which the combinatorial explosion of neuronal connections needed to be kept under control by prioritising stimuli that call for immediate action, pain proved an efficacious alarm system to get organisms out of harmful situations, though it had the perfectly useless characteristic of persisting after the danger had passed and of supervening even when the animal can do nothing about it (think of the toothache that elderly elephants suffer). About 50 million years ago, there evolved animate beings with brains able to concentrate their attention so as to derive pleasure from features of their environment, such as food. This development seems not to carry any survival advantage: these animals are rewarded with pleasure for doing what they do under the necessity of their basic drives, and the effect of stimulation of the dopaminergic system may have the disadvantage of distracting from biological needs. The relation between pleasure and the activities that give rise to it is a mere by-product of the adaptive development of superior intelligence; and animate beings that are capable of it may prefer pleasure to survival. In short, there was a lapse of perhaps a hundred million years in which there was pain on Earth and no pleasure. This gives us one very strong sense in which they are not opposite states of a single bodily apparatus.

Of course, neither Eudoxus nor, even less, Aristotle had the slightest inkling of what we have just sketched, and probably would not have believed it in the form presented. Yet these physiological and ergonomic facts have scarce, if any, bearing on the axiological thesis that they wished to support in the face of

Speusippus' perversity. That is, they are interested in the value of pleasure, rather than in its generation.

6.2 Speusippus and the Neutral State

Speusippus and other followers of Plato were notorious in antiquity for maintaining not merely the Stoic-flavoured thesis that pain is an 'indifferent' in the sense sketched above (Section 5.2), but that both pleasure and pain are evils opposed to each other (e.g. Aulus Gellius 1927, IX.5).[8] We have already described this view as fanatical and perverse. But it does not come from nowhere and, because he was Plato's successor as head of the Academy, Speusippus deserves at least a summary hearing. Diogenes Laertius reports in his life of Speusippus (IV.4) that he wrote a book specifically about pleasure and one, presumably critical, about the (quasi-)hedonist Aristippus; but these, like all his other voluminous writings, have (perhaps thankfully) been lost, so we have to rely on Aristotle's report of the cut-and-thrust between him and Eudoxus to get a flavour of his argumentation.

Relative to the two reports of Eudoxus' *Opposites* argument cited above, Aristotle carries slightly different versions of Speusippus' objections.

In book VII, the objection is couched in mathematical terms. The principle on which it rests is that the more is opposed to the less and both are opposed to the equal (*EN* VII.12 1153b5–7). The intermediate state of the equal stands between the two extremes. On this scheme, even if pain is an evil, pleasure may be so too, because it too is opposed to the intermediate state of harmony, which is the opposite of both pain and pleasure.

This three-termed understanding of opposition may put us in mind of the passage in the *Philebus* (32a) where Socrates notes that the too-hot and the too-cold are both opposed to the natural state of a living body. Likewise, on Aristotle's own theory of the virtues, the extremes of foolhardiness and cowardice are opposed to courage as the mean, and those of dissipation and insensibility are opposed to temperance as the mean. Perhaps it is on this account that Aristotle concedes that the structure Speusippus is appealing to is sound enough, but does not apply to the case in hand (*EN* X.2 1173a8–9). It does not apply because it is quite unclear both what the intermediate or neutral state between pleasure and pain is supposed to be and why this should be accounted a good.

As reported in book X, Speusippus' objection to Eudoxus' *Opposites* argument is not so much that the intermediate state between two extremes that are

---

[8] For reservations about Aulus' independence and reliability as a source and much other perceptive discussion of the dialectical position, see Warren 2009, esp. pp. 274 *et seq.*

evils is a good, as that it may itself be a thing to be avoided: if both pleasure and pain were in the class of evils, both would of necessity be to be avoided. It is less than certain whether the doctrine on offer should really be attributed to Speusippus (who is not mentioned by name in this passage) or the guise under which it appears in the text is an artefact of authorial impatience. In either case, Aristotle cuts through the jumble by appealing to the observable fact (*phainomenon*) that people avoid pain as evil and choose pleasure as good (*EN* X.2 1173a11–2); so it is in this axiological respect that they are opposites. That is to say, the opposition is two- rather than three-term, and the echoes of Socrates, on the natural bodily state or the opposition between excess and defect relative to the mean in connection with the virtues, are out of place.

In the foregoing pages, we have already mentioned Speusippus by name more times than Aristotle does in the whole of the *Corpus*. Apart from a glancing reference to his paralysis in old age (*Rhet.* III.10 1411a21), mentioned also by Diogenes (IV.3), there are two passages in the *Metaphysics* that associate him with the more mystical side of Platonic number theory (VII.2 1028b21 and XII.7 1072b31), which is also recalled in *EN* (I.6 1096b7). But he appears as proposing that pleasure is an evil only in the discussion in *EN* VII to which we have already referred.

From the fleetingness of his appearances in Aristotle's writings, we might suppose that Aristotle thought almost as ill of Speusippus as he did of Xenocrates (mentioned only four times in the *Corpus*), who succeeded him as head of the Academy and of whom Diogenes reports that Aristotle said that it is shameful to keep silence and let Xenocrates speak (V.3). Some of this rancour may be due to Aristotle's not having been nominated to succeed Plato as Scholarch.

But, in the particular case of Speusippus' stand on pleasure, there may be two more respectable factors in play. One is that, as has been emerging, Aristotle is happy to subscribe to the principle of *Opposites*: 'the opposed pains are evil; indeed, the opposite of an evil is a good' (*EN* VII.14 1154a12) and 'it is as good and evil that they [sc. pleasure and pain] are opposed' (*EN* X.2 1173a12–3). That is to say, Speusippus' objection to Eudoxus' hedonism is misguided. The other point is that we are informed by the occasionally credible Diogenes not only that Speusippus committed suicide rather than suffer disease but also that he was a 'liable to be dominated by pleasures' (IV.3 and 1 respectively). Not merely misguided, but insincere, while, as we have seen, the hedonist Eudoxus was in control of himself in his cultivation of the pleasures that suited him.

6.3 The Opposite of An Evil Is a Good

At the risk of oversimplifying, we may schematise the dialectical position as follows:

(i) Eudoxus' thesis: pleasure is the good;

(ii) First support for (i): all animate beings by nature aspire to pleasure (*Cradle* argument to be considered in the next section);

(iii) Second support for (i): the converse of (ii) is that pain is naturally to be avoided;

(iv) Principle of opposites: the opposite of what is naturally to be avoided is good;

(v) Specific opposites: pleasure is the (axiological) opposite of pain;

(vi) *Opposites*: (i) follows from (iii), (iv) and (v);

(vii) Speusippus' objection: supposing that (iv) is generalisable, then, given that both pleasure and pain are opposites of the intermediate, Eudoxus cannot argue from the badness of pain to the goodness of pleasure;

(viii) Aristotle's first reply to Speusippus: (iv) correctly captures the relation between pleasure and pain, so (v) is correct and (vii) is sophistical;

(ix) Aristotle's second reply: no one can (honestly) say that pleasure is an evil.

Of course, Aristotle's rejection of Speusippus' criticism of *Opposites* does not commit him to endorsing Eudoxus' full-blown hedonist thesis (i), but only the weaker claim, which is more clearly the aim in *EN* VII than in X, that pleasure is a good. But it is consistent with the thesis that, *as such*, pleasure is a good, even if the argument gives no indication of how to estimate the good of any given pleasure relative to other goods nor any strong reason to think that pleasure is in some way a dominant intrinsic good.

7 Cradle

7.1 Natural Tendencies

The impetus of the Eudoxan argument that we call *Cradle* makes itself felt in the very first lines of Aristotle's *Nicomachean Ethics*:

> Every art and every enquiry, just like every activity and choice, is said to aim (*ephiesthai*) at some good, so it has been well said that the good is that at which all things aim (*ephietai*). (*EN* I.1 1094a1–3)

We have indicated the Greek for the verb that we have rendered as 'to aim' in part because it covers a broad semantic field, from a sense of sending or (directed) throwing to that of aspiring or desiring. In Plato, it appears to denote craving (*Phil.* 20d8), or a tending to a higher good (*Phdr.* 237d9) and, in a passage we have already alluded to (Section 2.1) at the beginning of *Republic* II, being drawn to the goods that are desired only for themselves (357b4). The near-synonym '*phero*' has the literal sense of carrying, and we shall see shortly (Section 7.4) how broadly this literal sense is taken when applied to the movements of Aristotle's (and Eudoxus') celestial bodies.

Likewise, there is the almost throwaway remark in *EN* VII (13 1153b25–6) in which Aristotle says that the fact that 'all animals and all humans pursue pleasure points to its being in some way (*pōs*) the best of things'. If there is some way in which pleasure might be the best of things, it may also be that there is some way in which it is not. Aristotle does not here spell out such another way, but we may reasonably guess what he has in mind is that the pursuit of pleasure somehow masks the pursuit of what he thinks is really the best of things, namely happiness (*eudaimonia*; cf. *EN* I.4 1095a18).

Though Eudoxus is not mentioned in the short passages just cited, it is again hard to think that he is not on Aristotle's mind. For the rather compressed argument they present is set out a little more fully when, in book X, Aristotle gives his rundown of Eudoxus' arguments in favour of pleasure. The longer version runs:

> He [*sc.* Eudoxus] saw that all animate beings, both rational and irrational, aim (*ephiemena*) at it [*sc.* pleasure], and he argued that in every case the object of choice is what is fitting and what is more so is best, and the fact that all are carried (*pheresthai*) to the same thing points to its being the best for all, since each thing finds its own good, just as with food; and he thought that what is good for all and what all aim at (*ephietai*) is the good. (*EN* X.2 1172b9–15)

We have supplied the word 'animate' in this rendering. This addition may be justified by considering that, for instance, a stone has a tendency toward the centre of the gravitational field in which it is located and ought to be counted as inanimate and, so, non-rational. But it is clear from the reference to choice that the argument has to do with ensouled or self-moving beings. In any case, we wanted to avoid the potentially theological overtones of 'creatures', and analogues in other languages, that some translators are at home with.

Our adoption of the label 'Cradle' for the argument just carried is a nod to a passage in Cicero's *De finibus* ('*ad incunabula*': V.20.55). In this text, Torquatus, the representative of Epicureanism, says that, of old, the members of his school appealed to the behaviour of children in the cradle as reflections of how things stand in nature ('*speculum naturæ*', II.10.32) and, so, the least corrupted and most reliable witnesses ('*incorrupti atque integri testes*' I.21.71) to determine the nature of the good. Given that the newborn choose pleasure and shun pain, the former is good and the latter evil.

While *Cradle*-type arguments of various sorts and with various outcomes were undoubtedly popular among the Hellenistic schools (see, again, Brunschwig 1986), there remain at least two problems with Cicero's attribution. One is that, as it is presented by Torquatus, the argument leaks worse than the Titanic on a bad day. And the other is that we have very poor grounds for attributing such an argument to Epicurus himself. But it would take us too far afield to go into these thorny matters.

More to our present purposes are two lexical choices in the passage from *EN* X that we have carried.

One is that Aristotle says that Eudoxus 'saw' (*horan*) a certain behaviour in all animate beings. Apart from exceptional cases, if I say that someone sees that *p*, then I am committed to saying that *p* is there to be seen. And this in turn commits me to allowing that *p*, unless I cite something exceptional about the case. Given that Aristotle does not say there was anything aberrant in Eudoxus' seeing, he seems to be conceding that a certain fact is there to be seen, namely that both rational and irrational animate beings tend towards pleasure. This, then, would be a factual or descriptive premise on which *Cradle* feeds. Even if the description is itself 'disputable' (Warren 2009, p. 260), it is not disputed by Aristotle in the passage we are considering.

The rather more evaluative premise, smuggled in perhaps as a sort of verbal synonymy, would be the passage from what is to be chosen (*haireton*) to what is beneficial (*epiekes*). But this connection is not just a value-judgement, which may be a take-it-or-leave-it matter. For, if the aside about animals' foods is Aristotle's contribution to making *Cradle* plausible, then it may be helpful to recall how, in the *History of Animals*, he takes it as read that different animals have different foods that are suited to them (e.g. *HA* VIII.1 589a4–10 and 590b10). For instance, a lion eats raw zebra while a panda eats lots of bamboo; and each can thrive in its own way given its eating habits (cf. Aufderheide 2020, pp. 62–3). Such correlations between the preferences of a given animal and what is good for it lie at the heart of Aristotle's teleological biology, which he seems to be bringing in aid of Eudoxus' argument, whether Eudoxus would have subscribed to it or not.

As what counts as food depends on what it is food for, so the pleasures of a given animate being will be adapted to its nature (cf. *EN* X.5 1176a5–10).

7.2 The Pleasures of Animals and Children

Putting on hold the neurological and palaeontological stories about the relations of pain to pleasure sketched in Section 6.1, we may interrogate a little more closely why the argument carried in Section 7.1 from *EN* X.2 makes reference to the tendencies not only of rational but also of irrational animate beings.

If the purest – most Epicurean – form of *Cradle* argument were that animals and children are uncorrupted and, so, reliable guides to the good, the quick answer would be to observe that animals and children are not reliable guides to anything. Even Lucretius, who repeatedly presents himself as being as faithful as he can to Epicurus, admits that babies are unprepared for life (*DRN*, V.222–34). Though a good Epicurean is sure that pleasure is the 'guide to life' (*dux vitæ*: II.172) and 'what we all tend to' (*quo tendimus omnes*: V.26), it is not from observing children that we can discern this. After all, it is not to infants that we appeal to corroborate such beliefs as we might entertain about infinitesimals, Byzantine architecture or fiscal accountancy.

If only animate beings that are devoid of reason (*anoeta*: *EN* X.2 1173a2) tended towards pleasure, then it would make sense to doubt that pleasure is good for animate beings in general. But, given that deliberating beings (*phronima*: *EN* X.2 1173a4) do so too, this can hardly be right. Though it is extravagant to suppose that animals are drawn to food for the pleasure of eating, it is not so very wild to see that, at least in some 'higher' animals, food is indeed – incidentally to its nutritive function – a source of pleasure.[9] These are pleasures of what we have been calling the *woohoo* variety, in which the perceptual faculty is, among other things, the capacity for pleasure and pain (*De An.* II.2 413b23–4, to which we return shortly).

As Mill reminds us in the second chapter of *Utilitarianism* (Mill 1861), many commentators, from Horace (*Ep.* iv 13) on down, have thought that pleasure is an end fit only for pigs, where a pig's pleasures will be primarily of the *woohoo* kind. Hence, the hedonist is one who thinks fit for humans what is properly fit for pigs. The accusation would be justified if (adult) humans were capable of only those pleasures that are fit for pigs. Though most humans are indeed capable of pigs' pleasures, and these may be considered, in the vocabulary that Mill himself uses, 'lower', they are not the only ones, as we have already indicated with our neologism of '*ahah*' pleasures.

One step up a supposed hierarchy of pleasures from lower to higher would be those that derive from play. Thus, both a dog and an infant can keep themselves amused for a while with a rag doll, and in very much the same ways. At a certain point, the repertoire of a dog's pleasures reaches a limit ('you can't teach an old dog new tricks'). By contrast, as the child grows, the range of things that it can be entertained by expands and these will tend not only to be less repetitious but also to become more elaborate. Moreover, the promise of a lower pleasure can be used to induce a child into acclimatising itself to higher pleasures: 'if you eat

---

[9] A friend, sensitive enough to be a professional art historian, claims to have seen a slug taking delight in munching through his basil plant. The empathy thus engendered saved the slug's life.

your spinach, you can have a sweet'; and, perhaps at a later stage: 'if you do your homework, you can go out to play' (hinted at by Aristotle at *EN* X.1 1172a21–3). Even if the higher occupation is not at the time a source of enjoyment for the child, the enhancement of its repertoire for appreciations may nurture its capacities for more satisfying pastimes. Of course, there is no guarantee that this sort of development will take place, nor that it will go very far. But it may be a start in the direction of increasingly *ahah* pleasures.

As we saw in considering *Witness*, in cases like that of Eudoxus himself, as a person matures, infantile pleasures lose at least some, if not all, of their appeal. Though the adult may find herself in complex relations with the lower pleasures, of the sort that give rise to phenomena of *akrasia*, so astutely dissected in the early chapters of *EN* VII, it is precisely because they are pleasures that they provoke the conflicted episodes in question: one is only tempted by what is tempting, even if one knows better.

7.3 Sensation and Appetite

In three short passages of the second book of *On the Soul*, Aristotle enunciates a series of theses that link the terms in play in what we are taking to be Eudoxus' version of *Cradle*. Though there are some tangles in each of these passages, we label them (A: *De An.*, II.2 413b22–5) (B: II.3 414b2–4) and (C: b12–14) and propose to unpick them with the following conditionals:

(i) If an organism has sensation (*aisthēsis*), it has appetite (*orēxis*) and is capable of both pleasure (*hēdonē*) and pain (*lupē*) (A and B)
(ii) If an organism has sensation, it has imagination (*phantasia*) (A)
(iii) If an organism has pleasure or pain, it has (of necessity) desire (*epithumia*) (A)
(iv) If an organism has appetite, it has desire, inclination (*thumos*) and wish (*boulēsis*) for pleasure (B)
(v) If an organism has hunger or thirst, it has desire (C)

From the conjunction of (i), (ii) and (iii), it follows that, if an organism has sensation, then it has imagination and desire, which seem to be the preconditions of its being moved to find food (cf. *MA* 6, 700b16–17 and 7, 701a33–4). From the conjunction of (i) and (iv), it follows that, if an organism has sensation, then it has a drive for pleasure. The tricky bit is the move from the references to hunger and thirst in (v) to those to pleasure and pain in (i) and (iii). And the trick would be to say that, if hunger and thirst are appetites, then their satisfaction just *is* the generation of pleasure. But Aristotle does not say this out loud; and, from (i)-(v), it looks as if it would be to affirm the consequent ('if p then q, and q; therefore p') to make this move.

Affirmation of the consequent was named (with the name '*epomenon*') and shamed as a sophistical manoeuvre by Aristotle himself (*Soph. El.* 5 167b1–20). But a majority of the examples that he gives of it are, on reflection, in pretty good argumentative shape (Davies 2020). It also appears to be the format in which some more recent commentators have cast their accounts of the role that pleasure is meant to play in explaining animal behaviour in such a way as to ensure their survival. Perhaps three instances will suffice to indicate how pervasive this tendency is. When a behavioural biologist subtitles a book 'The Science of Pleasure' and asks, 'what is pleasure for?', he replies, citing natural selection as his explanatory framework, that '[p]leasure entices us to behave in ways that are likely to be biologically beneficial' (Martin 2008, p. 15). When a neurologist writes a book to explain the cerebral and neurological bases of 'the pleasure center', he summarises his opening chapter by saying that '[p]leasure can be defined as a way of fulfilling the evolutionary imperatives of survival and procreation' (Kringelbach 2009, p. 10). And, when an eminent psychologist aims to explain 'why we like what we like', he starts with what we have already heard from Aristotle: '[a]nimals need water to survive, and so they are motivated to seek it out. Pleasure is the reward for getting it; pain is the punishment for doing without' (Bloom 2010, p. 4).

These seem to be just the ticket to get the conclusion that Eudoxus would like to draw from the Aristotelian theses (i)–(v), namely that pleasure is the good that organisms are naturally carried toward with a view to their survival. The trouble, however, is that, despite the authors' asseverations, there is hardly anything evolutionistic about the three views just canvassed. As any moderately orthodox Darwinian will tell you, natural selection has to do not with individuals, but with species or genes. And these, considered as abstract objects rather than organisms, are not proper subjects of pleasure or pain. The 'reward' for doing what is beneficial is not pleasure but the reproduction of the species or the transmission of genes; and the 'punishment' is not pain but extinction.

Of course, Eudoxus, and still less Aristotle, would be little impressed by the observation that what we have cited from our modern scientists is not Darwinian orthodoxy. Indeed, they might be gleeful that, when it comes to such things as pleasure, the final causation that Darwin sought to expel from the explanation of animal behaviour returns through the back door to supply the crucial premise for a *Cradle* argument. And this is what Eudoxus 'saw' (*EN* X.2 1172b10) and 'said well' (*EN* I.1 1094a2).

7.4 A Teleological Principle and the Celestial Intelligences

In the preceding sections, we have been considering the pleasures that humans share with other animals, but in Section 3.2, we introduced a caricature distinction between those pleasures, which we called '*woohoo*', that have given hedonism a bad name because associated with cattle (*EN* I.5 1095b20, cited in Section 5.3) and pigs (Horace) and those, which we called '*ahah*', that are the only sort that a creature with no bodily appetites, such as an angel, would recognise as such, though they are also available to many humans and perhaps a few 'higher' animals. The terminology proposed by Mill of 'higher' and 'lower' pleasures has the advantage of allowing a gradation, rather than a hard-and-fast difference in kind, but it may have the disadvantage of downplaying the distinctiveness of pleasures that are generated by the filling of a biological lack and those that are less so. While want of food causes pain, the absence of occasions for contemplation may provoke nothing worse than frustration.

The bioscientists cited in the previous section seem to converge on the notion that pleasure must have some aim or purpose: it is unabashedly teleological in nature. If a certain organism's behaviour is to be explained, it will be so at least in part with reference to the satisfaction of some desire. Without going so far as to identify pleasure with desire-satisfaction, we can make out some sort of correlation between the desires an organism can entertain and the pleasures of which it is capable. We gestured at play as one step 'up' from the bovine/porcine *woohoo* pleasures such as that of eating, which are in the first instance satisfactions of needs, but may also respond to desires. Moreover, the sorts of play to which a given organism can devote itself may be graded according to the level of behavioural sophistication of which the organism is capable. Hide-and-seek should count as lower than chess, so to say.

The tendency to expand the repertoire of an organism's pleasures may be described as 'superteleological', which may be what Aristotle is hinting at in the comment at *EN* X.2 1173a4–5, where the idea seems to be that an organism of level n may tend (once again, the verb is *ephiemi*) towards pleasures of level $n+1$. And some such principle is in play in the discussion of the sources of human happiness in *EN* I.9 (1099b 13–7), according to which, even if it is won by effort and practice, it is to be counted among divine things.

Thus far, we have been paying attention mostly to the passages among the levels of pleasure that are closest to the *woohoo* end of the scale. But, if we can take Aristotle's reference to the divine seriously, we may also make out some of the characteristics of the more *ahah* kinds. This will leave rather unresolved how to rank the intermediate pleasures to which we have made reference (such as joking and puzzle-solving: Section 3.1). But, if we can get a grip on the good-making qualities of the more *ahah* pleasures, then we may understand better why a mathematician and astronomer like Eudoxus could also be a hedonist. For, picking up on the tripartition of the 'lives' in *EN* I.5 (1095b15–22; cited in Section 5.3), Aristotle dedicates X.7 to a rundown of the characteristics of the pleasures to be had from the life of contemplation (*biōs theorētikos*).

The highest virtue will be activity in accordance with the best part of ourselves, which Aristotle identifies as intellect (*nous*: *EN* X.7 1177a14), though he havers a little over whether this is actually divine or just the most divine aspect of humans (a16–7). A related rumination occurs near the end of the chapter (1177b28–32), where what have called superteleology is in play: even if the activity of the intellect has something of the divine about it, it is proper for humans to pursue it as superior to their nature as beasts.

The activity proper to the intellect is contemplation. Aristotle does not say here what the objects of this contemplation should be beyond their being the highest things (1177a20–1), but it is a fair guess that he has in mind just such studies as mathematics and astronomy insofar as they concern the stablest of things. This activity is the most continuous of which humans are capable (a22–3), and is also the most pleasurable because the pleasures are wonderfully pure and enduring (a25–6). They are pure because, unlike most *woohoo*-type pleasures, they do not presuppose some preceding lack and are thus self-sufficient (a28). Moreover, the person who cultivates this activity can (but need not) do so alone and is also in this respect the most self-sufficient (*autarkestatos*: 1177b1). While most other activities aim at some end outside themselves, contemplation is loved for its own sake (b3) and it is an end subserved by other activities, such as business and politics; it is therefore a sort of leisure (*scholē*: b5).

We may note *en passant* how much more sophisticated Aristotle is in picking out what makes a given pleasure desirable than what we glanced at in considering Bentham in Section 3.2. With his rundown of the good-making characteristics of contemplation, Aristotle must be presupposing not only that it can be praised in light of the quantity and quality of the pleasure it procures, but also that, up to a certain point, the pleasure so procured cannot itself be praised.

That point is reached when the highest human pleasures are considered in comparison with what they aspire to: the pleasures fit for the celestial beings considered in *Metaphysics*, XII (esp. 7 and 8). Like the angels that we have appealed to several times, Aristotle's Prime Mover and the unmoved movers of the heavens do not have sensation, but they do have appetite or desire (*to orekton*: *Metaph.* XII.7 1072a26) and pleasure (1072b17); but, having no body (1072a8–11), they have neither hunger nor thirst. Because they have a rational soul, they count as living beings (*zōa*: 1072b29–30) that are dedicated to two activities: one is to cause the movement of the celestial spheres considered as the objects of their love (1072b3–4); and the other is contemplation, specifically contemplation of themselves (1072b16–20). Given that this latter activity is in itself desirable (*di auto haireton*: 1072a35), the life of these beings is itself pleasurable (1072b16). Indeed, in the following lines, where Aristotle expresses himself with uncustomary warmth, he repeatedly says that this life is the most pleasurable (*hēdiston*: 1072b17, b24[10]) and so all the better and more marvellous (*thaumasiōteron*: b26).

If the teleological principle indicates that the end for which a being undertakes an activity is its good, then it emerges that, for the celestial beings, pleasure is the end of their contemplation; so pleasure is the good for the gods. Likewise, the superteleological principle indicates that if the highest good for humans is the good of the beings higher than them, then a certain pleasure is the highest good for them. If pleasure is good enough for the gods, then it's good enough for me.

Aristotle's accounts of these matters, as we have tried to convey them (albeit summarily), are to be found in texts close to his discussions of Eudoxus on pleasure and of Eudoxus on the heavenly bodies. So might we not suppose that Eudoxus is at least at the back of his mind in this theorising?

8 End

8.1 Choosing Things for Themselves

We come, then, to the sixth of the arguments Aristotle associates with Eudoxus' defence of his hedonistic doctrine. As indicated in Section 1.3, *End* comes at the end of our sequence because it presents itself as being strong in two senses: it is ambitious in the claim it aims to support; and, even in the telegraphic version that Aristotle gives of it, it is not easy to dismiss. The pith of it is as follows:

> that is most desirable which we choose not because of or for the sake of something else; as everyone agrees, this is pleasure; for we never ask someone what is the aim of his enjoyment, as if pleasure in itself is to be chosen (*EN* X.2 1172b20–3).

We heard in Section 6 the likes of Speusippus trying to disagree with what everyone else agrees about. But we found that the grounds on which that disagreement was built are very shaky indeed. We shall return to illustrate one way in which such an attempt to disagree can be embarrassed in much the terms that *End* is couched in. First, however, we may look a little more closely at the genealogy and the structure of the argument.

---

[10] The theme is taken up by Iamblichus in a text regarded by Ross as testimony for Aristotle's *Protrepticus* (fr. 14).

In Section 2.1, we made glancing reference to the beginning of the second book of Plato's *Republic* (357B4-D2), where Glaucon and Socrates are sorting the categories of goods. The tripartition they converge on may be expressed in modern terms as one that distinguishes 'pure ends', 'means-and-ends' and 'mere means'. As noted, Glaucon places in the class of things that are chosen for themselves, and not in view of anything else, enjoyment (*to chairein*) and innocent pleasures (*hēdonai ablabeis*). Like *Honour* discussed in Section 5, neither Glaucon's taxonomy nor, as it stands, *End* gives us strong reason to think that pleasure is the only thing that is not desired in view of some other good. Yet, such a uniqueness thesis would seem to be called for to back the claim that hedonism is a complete account of pure ends.

We might make this problem more explicit by considering a plausible rival to pleasure in the category of pure ends. Such a rival would be the happiness or flourishing (or, at an etymological stretch, good fortune) that Aristotle calls '*eudaimonia*'. Where pleasure might be the end of individual choices and actions, *eudaimonia* is rather a characteristic of a life as a whole (including, indeed, one's reputation after death: *EN* I.9). Thus, Aristotle is free to say that pleasure may be chosen for itself at any given stage in life, and that a life without pleasure is not worth living, but he might insist that what makes a life truly fulfilled is that it has a satisfactory overall shape. This, may, after all, be a true evaluation of the position; but Eudoxus is equally free to say that it is hard to see how one can *aim* at such an architectonic outcome (cf. *EN* I.1 1094a27), because each of our choices has to do with the options available to us from moment to moment.

Setting ourselves long-term projects, such as understanding the movements of the heavenly bodies, may generate enduring pleasures, but such are the vicissitudes of life that we cannot *choose* to be happy and flourishing. For instance, we may suppose that the fall from grace of Eudoxus' father after the Athenian takeover of Cnidus set limits to the good that Eudoxus could do in his home city, as well as to his comfort on his first visit to Athens. And much the same might be said of Aristotle's own prudent withdrawal from the city in 323 BCE with the death of Alexander. Insofar as *eudaimonia* depends, at least in part, on good luck, the extent to which we are in a position to cultivate it is not entirely in our power.[11]

---

[11] For present purposes, we may put to one side the tormenting and pressing questions of the contingency of the circumstances of one's birth, starting with location, gender and class, and hence, of the opportunities that are open or closed in making one's way through life.

8.2 Hierarchies of Choice

As presented above, *End* rests on an ordered hierarchy of the things that are chosen. If we permit ourselves a little formal abstraction, we may say that the ordering principle of this hierarchy is irreflexive, asymmetric and transitive. By irreflexiveness we mean that, if x is chosen but not for itself, then there must be some y such that x is chosen in view of y, and x and y cannot be identical. Asymmetry requires that, if x is chosen in view of y, then y cannot be chosen in view of x. And transitivity is the characteristic of the hierarchy that requires that, if x is chosen in view of y and y is chosen in view of z, then x is chosen in view (albeit indirectly) of z. Thus, if pleasure is chosen not in view of anything else, and other things are chosen in view of pleasure, then pleasure is as choosable as can be. If our remarks are sound about the Platonic tripartition of goods and about the most plausible rival of pleasure (Aristotle's *eudaimonia*), then it seems fair to conclude that pleasure is not merely an end, but the purest end.

In the first book of *Nicomachean Ethics*, Aristotle devotes considerable attention to the question that we are expressing in terms of means and ends. Though he is aiming for the conclusion that *eudaimonia* is the final end, in I.1 he subscribes to the view that means and ends form chains that are transitive and asymmetrical: the art of making bridles subserves the art of horse-riding, which in turn can subserve the arts of war (I.1 1094a10–5); it is left tacit, perhaps because too obvious, that no one goes to war in order to justify the making of bridles. The following chapter sets out from the idea that such chains are irreflexive (I.2 1094a19–23) and adds parenthetically the idea that they must also have a final term: 'we do not choose everything in view of something else (which would carry us to infinity, as every appetite [*orexis*] would be empty and vain)' (I.2 1094a20–1). Though he later says of *eudaimonia* that 'it is a principle [*archē*]: it is view of it that we do everything else, and it is the principle [*archē*] and cause of goods' (I.12 1102a 2–3), a doubt might be raised about how we can be sure that our appetites are not, in the end, 'empty and vain'.

For readers of German philosophy, there is ample repetition in Schopenhauer of the view that, even if all our wants were satisfied, we would still be at a loss (Schopenhauer 1820, and 1851, esp. vol. II, §152 on the unsatisfactoriness of Cockaigne); likewise the striking opening paragraph of Nietzsche's 'On Truth and Lies [*etc.*]', according to which the whole of human history is nothing but a futile minute before extinction (Nietzsche 1873, p. 369; on which see Davies 2018). For readers of Italian literature, the idea that all our desires are ultimately unavailing will be associated with the name of Giacomo Leopardi: even when we get what we want, what we will be left with will be boredom ('*noia*': e.g. Leopardi 1824 p. 146; 1826 pp. 226–7; and 1831, XXIV, ll. 25–43). And for readers of Russsian literature, the recurrent figure of the 'superfluous man', such as Lermontov's Pechorin (Lermontov 1840), will evoke the idea that it is senseless – or, at best, naïve – to pursue any goal in earnest. Of course it's not just a nineteenth-century thing: from the book of *Ecclesiastes* (1:2–3) down to the gloomier existentialistically inclined youth of today, the theme that all is vanity has been played in many variations. But we may label it 'the Romantic Challenge' to the idea of a hierarchy of values that, for Eudoxus and Aristotle, has a top level that makes life worth living.

We may consider three main dimensions of the Romantic Challenge. First, there is a question of scale: none of the things that count for me can be raised to the status of a value for the universe. Second: the transitoriness of human affairs means that nothing I achieve will have lasting value. And, third, there is the idea that, even once a given desire is satisfied, we cannot remain even briefly satisfied with that satisfaction. In each of these dimensions, the Romantic Challenge seems to presuppose that, in some sense, only the abstract or permanent can have authentic value, while the concrete and temporary is illusory or delusive.

Whether it be pleasure or *eudaimonia* that responds to the Challenge, it may be worth trying to deflate the appeal that Challenge undoubtedly exercises, so as to leave room for there being an overall goal to human activity: one that is chosen for itself and in view of which other things may be choosable.

Perhaps a first thing to query is the Romantic notion of a disproportion between my aspirations and the lack of response to them by a mute and indifferent world. For, 'the point of view of the universe' is not a position occupied by anyone, but is a mere abstraction, and it is quite arbitrary to privilege it over mine or anyone else's. For my actions to make sense for me it is not necessary that they be of universal significance. Nor yet that they be enduring: the fact that my affairs are transitory and few of my doings will leave much trace after my death does not mean that they do not count for me today. It seems to be mere prejudice to think that only what is permanent can have value. As we have already heard from Eudoxus and Aristotle, those pleasures that are naturally apt to be enduring, which are mostly of the *ahah* sort, make for greater overall satisfaction, not least because they are minimally dependent on contingent circumstance. But to say that they are nugatory because fleeting by comparison with the history of the universe seems quite unmotivated. Likewise, the Challenge that leads Leopardi to talk so much (and so boringly) of boredom – that the satisfaction of a desire does not bring satisfaction – appears to presuppose that we are doomed in some way to be spectators on our own affairs, rather than participants in them. After all, not all pleasures derive from the elimination of desire, and many of the most valuable involve our being engrossed in activities that fully occupy our attention, whether it be in playing a sport, fixing a motorbike or contemplating the heavenly bodies.

It may also be worth considering briefly a sort of converse of the Romantic Challenge. This we might label the Utilitarian Expansion. While the classical utilitarians, including both Bentham and Mill in their rather different ways, held that pleasure is the unique member of the class of pure ends insofar as it makes no sense to ask why one seeks it (cf. also *EN* X.2 1173b 21–4), the Expansionists take it that we should enlarge the class to include also other goods.

By way of example, we may cite John C. Harsanyi, winner in 1994 of the prize in memory of Alfred Nobel for Economics, who self-described as a utilitarian in many of his published writings.[12] In an article on individual utility and utilitarian ethics (Harsanyi 1986), Harsanyi fires off a list of goods that he seems to be treating as things that are desired for themselves. Though he does not himself make reference to the Platonic tripartition, Harsanyi contemplates among pure ends success, money, love, friendship and respect (Harsanyi 1986, p. 3). We may note in passing that this listing does not include the commonplace candidates for the status of basic needs, such as nutrition, shelter and the chance to reproduce. But, as presented, Harsanyi's Expansion does not stand up under scrutiny.

Success. If this is taken generically to be the opposite of failure, then we may allow that it is preferable come what may. As such, it is not an object of desire or choice, but is rather an extrinsic characteristic of the upshots of the choices we might make from time to time. But it may be that the Utilitarian Expansion means something more substantial, such as winning a Nobel Prize and influencing a generation of economists. Taken this way, it would seem that the good acquired – the prestige – is a means to satisfactory outcomes.

Money. This Expansion is unworthy even of an economist: money cannot be other than a means, as Aristotle definitively illustrated a couple of millennia ago (*Pol.* I.9).

Love. Again an ambiguity. An unrequited love may well be a source of affliction. And being loved by a pest likewise. It is not the emotive state that is desired for itself, but its more fortunate effects (including pleasure).

Friendship. While certain reciprocal interpersonal relationships are surely integral to a satisfactory life, it seems rather that it is the satisfaction that confers value on them.

---

[12] Indeed, a collection of translations of his articles into Italian goes under the title '*L'utilitarismo*' (Harsanyi 1995).

Respect. Like the esteem owing to a Nobel laureate, the respect of one's peers may contribute to self-esteem. But this is desired for the peace of mind that it brings.

Though our treatment of the suggested Expansion is perhaps over-brutal, it remains hard to see how a consistent utilitarian can expand the class of pure ends much beyond what Glaucon pointed to, and to which Eudoxus seems to be subscribing in the argument we are calling *End*.

8.3 Against a Regress of Chosen Ends

In addition to Aristotelian eudaimonism, what we have been calling the Romantic Challenge and the Utilitarian Expansion propose rivals to the hedonistic thesis that pleasure is intrinsically valuable because unique in being desired for itself, as a pure end and not in view of anything else. The former says that nothing is intrinsically valuable; and the latter that other things are desired for themselves. We have made a stab at discrediting these rivals; but this is a rather negative defence of the Eudoxan position summed up in *End*.

To be a little more propositive, we may hazard a pincer movement to insinuate, on the one hand, just how quickly sequences of means and ends arrive at a reference to pleasure, and on the other, just how potent the arrival point is as a motivation. Though neither of these manoeuvres is strictly required in defence of *End* and they are not to be found (for reasons that should become clear) in the ancient literature, the hope is that they will make plain why Eudoxus' argument, even in the summary version we find in Aristotle, is more cogent than it may look at first glance.

We borrow the first claw of our pincer from Sir David Hume, whose *Enquiry Concerning the Principles of Morals* first appeared in 1751 and was polished in the posthumous edition that is generally taken to be authoritative (Hume 1777). In the fifth section of the first appendix (§244), Hume defends the thesis that the ultimate ends of human action 'cannot be accounted for by *reason*' (emphasis original) or 'the intellectual faculties'. The view Hume is opposing may thus be called 'Rationalism' to group together some theologically motivated views doing the rounds in eighteenth-century England and Scotland. In this polemic, Hume deploys two specular arguments: one to show that the avoidance of pain is 'an ultimate end' and the other to show that pleasure must be 'desirable on its own account'. Hume presents these arguments in quasi-dialogical form, with rather unruly use of italics for the two voices in play; but we may make the back-and-forth more explicit by presenting the opposed positions as put into the mouths of Hume and the Rationalist, as follows.

1. *The hatefulness of pain*

    H: Why do you use exercise?

    R: Because I desire to keep my health.

    H: Why do you desire health?

    R: Because sickness is painful.

    H: Why do you hate pain?

    R: Because it is painful and I can give no reason beyond that.

2. *The desirability of pleasure*

    H: Again, why do you desire health?

    R: It is necessary for the exercise of my calling.

    H: Why are you anxious on that head?

    R: Because I desire to get money.

    H: Why do you desire money?

    R: Because it is the instrument of pleasure.

    H: Why do you desire pleasure?

    R: It is an absurdity to ask for a reason for that.

It may be that, in some moods, Plato contemplates views that could be assimilated to the sort of Rationalism that Hume has in his sights. But it is hard to think of any contemporary interlocutor of Aristotle or Eudoxus who could be a target of the lines of thought that invite exchanges like *The hatefulness of pain* and *The desirability of pleasure*. In this sense, our appeal to Hume has an air of anachronism about it. But, they do seem to illustrate what Hume wished to illustrate, namely that the Rationalist runs out of reasons for her choices and must at some point concede the intrinsic badness of pain and the intrinsic goodness of pleasure. Moreover, these little dialogues may help to bring into focus two facets of the Eudoxan argument we are considering.

One is how very quickly the hatefulness of pain and the desirableness of pleasure can be made explicit under this sort of interrogation. Even if there may be several phases in the regress in the giving of reasons for certain preferences, the notion that such a regress may be infinite is very implausible. Naturally, the Rationalist may go in for some delaying tactics, for instance, saying that she wants money to go on holiday to Barbados, to lie on the beach in the sun drinking piña colada. But Hume can still ask why she wants to do that, and sooner or later the Rationalist will give the exasperated reply that he is after: she will end up saying that it is an absurdity to ask for a reason for desiring pleasure.

The other facet is that, though 'Why do you desire money?' and 'Why do you desire pleasure?' share the same surface form, the former admits of a sensible answer but the latter does not. This, we take it, is the point of Aristotle's attribution to Eudoxus of the idea that 'we never ask someone what is the aim of his enjoyment' (*EN* X.2 1172b22), which is the key move in *End* as we cited it above. Of course Aristotle could still say that 'Why do you pursue *eudaimonia*?' is likewise a senseless question (*EN* I.4 1095a18). But we have already suggested that, though *eudaimonia* will be characteristic of a globally satisfactory life, it does not look like the sort of thing one can choose from moment to moment.

As with the neurological and paleontological 'Just-So' stories evoked in Section 5.1, the second claw of our pincer movement against the threat that pleasure is not an or the ultimate end for humans invokes some empirical findings that Eudoxus could hardly have dreamt of. Indeed, insofar as these discoveries concern primarily pleasures of what we have been calling the *woohoo* sort, he might even have been disconcerted or disappointed by them, given his own inclinations in favour of the *ahah*.

The starting-point of the present 'Just-So' story is what mice can be made to do. Two Canadian psychologists found that a mouse will prefer the application of a weak electrical current to the zone of the amygdala known as the *nucleus accumbens* to any offer of food, drink or sex (Olds and Milner 1954). If the mouse is allowed freely to self-stimulate in this way by activating a lever, it will continue to do so and will allow itself to die of hunger and thirst (and will have no offspring): the appetite for stimulation of the *nucleus accumbens* is never sated. When an analogous procedure was applied to humans, the subjective accounts given of the experience varied from that of relaxation and optimism to that of orgasmic euphoria (Heath 1963). Some proper scruple (which might also have been applied to mice) seems to have prevented the experimenters from seeing whether humans would go the whole hog and effectively commit suicide in order to prolong the pleasure. But some studies have associated this sort of stimulation with the self-destructive tendencies of smokers, drinkers and drug users, as well as players of video games (respectively, Barrett 2004, Boileau 2003, Lamb 1991 and Koepp 1998). As we might expect from our treatment of *Opposites*, as regarding only questions of value and not of causation, activation of the *nucleus accumbens* does not relieve pain or reduce depression, although some deep-brain stimulation can mitigate certain sorts of pain that are otherwise hard to treat, such as those assigned to phantom limbs (Kringelbach 2007).

The 'Just-So' extension of these empirical findings would be this. Suppose some scientist stumbled on a cerebral location for the pleasures of geometry. If so, its electrical stimulation should satisfy Eudoxus, even if he makes no actual headway with geometry.

One thing that makes such a supposition rather disconcerting is the fact, to which we have already alluded, that the pleasure of eating is auxiliary or subordinate to the purpose of nutrition, while the more *ahah* pleasures do not display this sort of means-end structure. Yet, if, as for Thomistic angels, the pleasure of contemplation does not require the discovery of new truths or techniques of calculation, it is not entirely clear what is amiss with its generation by artificial means. If, that is, *End* is to be embraced consistently, then Eudoxus should attribute positive value to states thus generated.

Another sort of objection that might be raised would be analogous to Nozick's argument from the unreality of the apparent mental states produced in his Experience Machine (Nozick 1974, pp. 42–5; also Putnam 1981, ch. 1). Following this tack, a brain that is artificially stimulated is not having any thoughts at all because they are not appropriately connected to what they appear to be about. While this might have some – albeit controversial[13] – purchase on the more *woohoo* pleasures, we seem to be free to think that the more *ahah* types, not being *causally* dependent on their objects (e.g. numbers and forms), are genuine enough even if their generation is somewhat deviant. If so, Eudoxus might find himself forced to concede that a simulated appreciation of Pythagoras' Theorem is still an appreciation of Pythagoras' Theorem. This would, of course, not be a comfortable concession because it is intuitive to suppose that the characteristically *ahah* pleasures should be in one way or another active: doings rather than undergoings. Moreover, the Nozickean scenario is a way of updating the Cartesian Demon, with all the complications that that entails (see Davies 2004). But, if the content of the simulation were the Theorem as it truly is, then, when I contemplate it, I really am grasping some geometry.

A more radical response that seems to be open to Eudoxus is to say that the hypothesis on which the 'Just-So' story depends is close to incoherent. While it might have been a surprise to find that there turns out to be just one site in the brain that is activated in diverse *woohoo* pleasures, the assumption that most *ahah* pleasures, such as those of contemplation or calculation, are more properly doings than undergoings would indicate that they cannot be simulated and retain their character as pleasures.

Though the mental processes involved, for instance, in twigging a winning chess move are undoubtedly cerebral, that does not imply that the pleasure of going through them need have a neurological location. If so, there need be no correlate of the *nucleus accumbens* for *ahah* pleasures, or even for any given variety of them. And this, in turn, would mean that we need not take the 'Just-So' story as a serious threat to Eudoxus' hedonism, with its emphasis on *ahah* pleasures, while respecting the scientific evidence for the powerful hold that

---

[13] See notes 1 and 2 of Belshaw 2014 for a variety of responses to Nozick.

woohoo pleasures have on us, irrespective of how they are generated, because, in both cases, we have to do with ends that make life worth living.

8.4 Pleasure Perfects Activity

In two chapters of *EN* X closely adjacent to that in which he reports Eudoxus' arguments for hedonism, Aristotle develops long discussions of the status and the varieties of pleasure (i.e. X.4 and 5 respectively). In the intervening chapter (X.3), he makes some general remarks about some misconceptions about the notion, such as that it is some sort of movement or generation (1173a30–2), or that bogus, infantile or shameful pleasures can make for a good life (1173b31–4a4), concluding that these observations indicate that pleasure is not the good (1174a8–9), although some pleasures are worthy of being chosen for themselves (a10).

While this guarded conclusion would seem to be enough to respond to Eudoxus' position, Aristotle re-opens the question of just what pleasure is by trying to explain in what respect it is complete or perfect. And, in the course of the two chapters in question, he repeatedly says or implies that it is (4: 1174a17, b6, b8–9, b13, b23–4, b32–3 and 5a16–7; 5: 1175a30, a35–6, b15–7, b30–1, b36–6a1 and a26–8). In taking this stand, he likens it to seeing and contrasts it with house-building and walking a certain distance (*EN* X.4, 1074a20-b6) and alludes (b3) to the discussion in the *Metaphysics* (IX.6 1048b18–35; also *Phys.*, III.1) that uses the same examples to make the point he is trying to bring out, at which we have already glanced in Section 4.4 in contrasting *kineseis* with *energeiai*. But exactly what the point is proves elusive; so much so that one illustrious commentator has diagnosed here 'serious confusion in Aristotle's exposition' of the distinction (Ackrill 1965, p. 135).[14] For present purposes, however, we may pick up on two observations that Aristotle is pretty clearly making, one towards the end of chapter 4 and the other in chapter 5.

The former takes off from the notion that life itself is a sort of activity (*EN* X.4 1175a12). To live life to the full is to exercise one's faculties; and it may well be with Eudoxus in mind that one of Aristotle's examples is the choice of the studious person (*philomathēs*: 1175a14) to devote himself to theoretical matters. For this reason, people have good reason to pursue pleasure because it perfects the life of each. And the conclusion he draws

---

[14] Indeed, the contested terms (*kinēsis* and *energeia*) have generated a huge amount of commentary: in their bibliography, Radice and Davies (1997) log 91 discussions of the former and 129 of the latter as they appear in the twentieth-century literature on the *Metaphysics*; many of those that discuss one term discuss also the other and the various ways of explicating Aristotle's distinction between them.

is that there is no pleasure without activity and no perfect activity without its pleasure (a20–1).

It remains unclear, however, how widely applicable this strong conclusion is to be taken, especially in light of how Aristotle regards passive, childish and vicious pleasures as hardly pleasures at all, because pleasurable only to the depraved (*EN* X.5 1176a23–4). In the terms we have been using, the argument would apply almost exclusively to pleasures of a predominantly *ahah* sort. Yet the other example Aristotle gives of a proper exercise of our faculties is that of listening to music (*EN* X.4 1175a13–4): though this may require concentration on what is heard, it is not itself productive of music. In this direction, someone might allow that a person who concentrates on playing snooker or puts art into maintaining motorcycles derives from such activities pleasure that is as genuine as can be. And this someone might even be Aristotle himself, going by his claim in the following chapter that those who work with pleasure do so better and with greater precision (*EN* X.5 1175a32–3), and, once more, the first example he gives is of the greater proficiency of someone who enjoys doing geometry: Eudoxus again?

The other point worth picking up regards the fact that, given that there are various sorts and sources of pleasures, these may come into conflict with each other in such a way that attention to one occludes the enjoyment of another. The first case of this that Aristotle offers is one in which a lover of music may be distracted from a philosophical discussion by the sound of the playing of a flute (*EN* X.5 1175b3–6). We thus have potential competition between two *ahah* pleasures, so that the pleasanter drives out the other (b9–10). But Aristotle also seems to contemplate a case in which the weak *ahah* pleasure of watching a play when it is performed badly is driven out by the decidedly *woohoo* pleasure of munching sweets by way of distraction (b13–15). One might say that, in such a case, what we have is, above all, a wasted afternoon, though it would have been worse had we had no sweets to hand. But the notion that a lower pleasure can trump a higher in certain circumstances would indicate that the hierarchy of classes of pleasure at which Aristotle gestures, with those of the intellect as the purest and those of taste as the least pure (1176a1–3), is by no means as rigid as some of his more puritanical remarks, such as those in X.3 noted above, might lead us to expect.

Overall, then, we might say that Aristotle is alive to the ways that even defective pleasures can be valuable *qua* pleasures, and not only to persons of defective character, but also in circumstances where there is nothing better on offer.

9 How Much Did Aristotle Accept from Eudoxus?

Because he is almost our only source for Eudoxus' ethical doctrine, it is not surprising that we have mentioned Aristotle almost as often as we have the declared subject of this Element. And because we have been treating him as a generally sympathetic or at least charitable witness to what he reports, we may have given the misleading impression that Aristotle himself is some sort of hedonist. Not merely misleading, but grossly misleading. Yet, his vastly more subtle and nuanced theory of the good for humans does indeed contemplate a pronounced and positive role for pleasure.

In trying to give an answer to the question in our section title, we run at least three risks. Perhaps the least is that of repeating what we have already said in connection with the individual arguments considered in the foregoing five sections. Somewhat greater is the risk of giving the impression that Aristotle's responses to Eudoxus' arguments exhaust what he has to say about pleasure. If we were to avoid this, we would have to write quite another book, perhaps with some title such as *Aristotle on Pleasure*. Though I have tried *ambulando* to indicate my debts to books and articles that do have similar titles, I have not dared to compete with those that already exist. But perhaps the greatest risk is that of not being in a position to respond to the objection that what these two men happened to say so long ago does not take us very far in understanding the nature and value of pleasure. Attempts to avoid such a criticism might take the form of a history of what many other people have said about pleasure or that of an exposition of my own views of the matter.[15] Without being in a position to meet such a criticism head-on, I have indicated my impression that what Aristotle attributes to Eudoxus does, as a matter of fact, anticipate in one way or another a goodly portion of the arguments that have, at least in the Western tradition, been adduced in favour of the doctrine of hedonism, as well as bringing to the surface possible misunderstandings of what that doctrine amounts to.

Perhaps an exemplary case of this last point emerges from what was diagnosed in our third section as Aristotle's possible misapprehension of the force of *Witness*. The Athenians admired Eudoxus' moderation and found it surprising that such a man should assert that pleasure is the good. For, the typical representatives of that sort of view, such as the Callicles who figures in Plato's *Gorgias*, propose that the generation of pleasure is by way of desire-satisfaction, where the desires are those that humans share with other animals: the 'fleshly' pleasures that we have been nicknaming '*woohoo*'.

---

[15] In lecture courses off and on since the late 1980s, I made stabs in each of these directions, before hitting on Eudoxus as a useful hook also for didactic purposes.

On the one hand, the sorts of people who get a name for being hedonists generally give that doctrine a bad name, because the pleasures they go for are of a base and ignoble sort. On the other, someone, such as Eudoxus (or John Stuart Mill), who subscribes to the doctrine but cultivates the more angelic or *ahah* pleasures does indeed do something to redeem hedonism's reputation. Aristotle himself, in describing moderation, says that the person who succeeds in cultivating it and, so, is less subject to animal drives 'abstains from fleshly pleasure and finds this abstinence itself pleasurable' (*EN* II.3 1104b5–6). For this reason, his slight sniffiness about the Athenians' admiration for Eudoxus at *EN* X.2 1172b15–8 (cited at the outset of Section 3.1) may be rather out of place, because the considerations in play are part and parcel of Aristotle's own account of moderation.

In the least adventurous understanding of it, *Witness* may boil down to the thought that Eudoxus' behaviour shows that the pursuit of pleasure is consistent with leading an admirable life. The next argument in the order in which we have considered them goes just a little further. *Addition* aims to show that pleasure increases the good of a good activity. Aristotle is pretty clear in *EN* X.3 and elsewhere that the generation of pleasure is quite insufficient to justify depraved or infantile actions. Moreover, justifications of this sort may be misguided because such pleasures may be pleasures only in name, as perhaps the case of the sadist illustrates. But, in II.3, he seems to see the point of *Addition* and accepts its legitimacy with reservations, placing it alongside the noble and the expedient as justified motives of action (1104b30–1).

But Eudoxus' rejoinder would be that, while we might praise the noble and the expedient because they are sources of pleasure, it would be hard to say that pleasure is praised for being either noble or expedient. This is the thrust of the argument that we have been calling *Honour*: pleasure must be a good of the highest rank because we are at a loss to find terms for praising it. And it seems from *EN* I.12 that Aristotle takes the point. The point is that, if our terms of evaluation form a hierarchy that is irreflexive, asymmetrical and transitive, then it looks as if a category that does not admit of being evaluated in light of some higher category will be at the top of the heap. So, while we may appeal to the pleasurableness of a certain activity as a way of praising it, there is no non-tautological (or otherwise ridiculous) way of praising pleasure. To use a verb that Peter Geach did his best to put (back) in circulation (Geach 1960), the only thing we can do is macarize it, which corresponds to Aristotle's verbal choice in *EN* I.12 (*makarizō*) for saying that pleasure is to be honoured or glorified.

While 'to macarize' is something of a joke verb, verbs for saying that a certain thing is evil are perhaps more common. Prominent among them would be 'to deprecate', and others with a prefix beginning with 'd', some of which are clearly privative, would be 'disapprove', 'disfavour', 'disesteem', 'denigrate' and so on. Each of these is typically used for things that cause pain, revulsion or discomfort. Regarding the only argument of Eudoxus that appears in both of the treatments of pleasure in *EN* (VII.13 and X.2), Aristotle allows that there is a sense in which pain is an opposite of pleasure. The sense in which it is so is a question of value ('axiological'). Even if there is no single bodily system of which pleasure and pain are opposed states, the fact that people avoid pain, unless in view of greater (e.g. long-term) pleasure, is a sign that it is neither a good nor, as Speusippus and some Stoics pretended to maintain, a matter of indifference. If pleasure is opposed in the axiological sense to the recognised evil of pain, then it is a good.

We are repulsed by pain. In cases of surprise, we at least flinch; in cases that are more enduring, we look for modes of alleviating the pain, whether by bodily posture or movement or by the assumption of analgesics or other cures. The 'we' here applies not only to adult humans, but also to children and other animate (but not necessarily rational) creatures. Not only do we, in this broad sense, avoid pain, as the Eudoxan argument from *Opposites* proposes, but we are naturally inclined to seek pleasures and to regard them as proper ends of our activity, as Aristotle seems to presuppose in the very opening lines of the *Nicomachean Ethics*.

The fact that pleasure is the common object of pursuit of living beings, from cradle to grave, is a strong indicator that it, however it manifests itself at the various levels of sophistication of the creatures that pursue it, pleasure is the good to which living beings are borne by nature. Given that, in *EN* I.1, Aristotle sets off from some principle of this sort, it is no surprise that, when he attributes it to Eudoxus in X.2, he raises no significant objection against the hedonist version of the *Cradle* argument. As noted in Section 7.1 'cradle' arguments were commonplace moves in favour of a variety of ethical positions in antiquity, but Aristotle seems to have seen the particular force of it in favour a doctrine that gives pride of place to pleasure. Even if he would himself say that the fulfilled and fulfilling life of *eudaimonia* is what we are ultimately after, this is not something that we have it in our power to choose because its attainment is subject to extraneous circumstances over which we may have little or no control.

When we do have at least some control over our actions and, thus, may be said to be making voluntary choices (*EN* III.1–5, pretty much *passim*), we set ourselves goals and work out ways of achieving them. Often enough, the means we have to adopt to get what we want involve effort and even pain. But their adoption is in view of what we have chosen for itself and for ourselves. Eudoxus' claim, in the argument that we have labelled *End*, is that the ultimate link in any sensible chain of means and ends will be some sort of pleasure. In *EN* X.2 and 4, Aristotle does not countenance any objection to this line of thought, so he may be said to have conceded the strongest argument for the strongest form of hedonism. But it bears repeating that telling the truth and nothing but the truth does not imply telling the whole truth. What the rest of the story is goes beyond the present review of the hedonism of Eudoxus of Cnidus.

References

Primary texts

Aristotle of Stagira – references to work title, book and chapter with page, column and line of I. Bekker ed. 1831–6; where a modern apparatus or translation is cited, this is listed under 'Modern Authors'; title abbreviations adopted:

Cat.: *Categories*
DI: *On Interpretation*
An. Pr.: *Prior Analytics*
An. Po.: *Posterior Analytics*
Top.: *Topics*
Soph El.: *Sophistical Refutations*
Phys.: *Physics*
De Caelo: *On the Heavens*
GC: *On Generation and Corruption*
De An.: *On the Soul*
MA: *On the Movement of Animals*
Metaph.: *Metaphysics*
EN: *Nicomachean Ethics*
EE: *Eudemian Ethics*
Pol.: *Politics*
Rhet.: *Rhetoric*
Poet.: *Poetics*

Aulus Gellius (1927) *Noctes Atticæ* (2 vols, ed. and tr. Eng.) J. C. Rolfe, Cambridge MA, Harvard University Press.

Cicero, Marcus Tullius (*Tusc.*) *Tusculanarum disputationum libri V* (ed.) M. Pohlenz, Leipzig, Teubner (reprint Amsterdam 1957).

(*Fin.*) *De finibus bonorum et malorum* (ed.) J. S. Reid, Cambridge, Cambridge University Press (reprint Hildesheim 1968).

Diogenes Laertius (DL, *Vitæ*):

(2013) ed., *Lives of the Eminent Philosophers*, T. Dorandi, Cambridge, Cambridge University Press.

(2018) tr. Eng., *Lives of the Eminent Philosophers*, P. Mensch (et al.), Oxford, Oxford University Press.

Epicurus of Samos (1887) *Epicurea*, ed. H. Usener, Leipzig, Teubner (reprint 2002).

Eudoxus of Cnidus (1966) *Die Fragmente des Eudoxos von Knidos*, ed. and comm., F. Lasserre, Berlin, De Gruyter (reprint 2011).

Iamblichus of Chalcis (1888) *In Nicomachi Arithmeticam Introductionem Liber*, ed. H. Pistelli, Stuttgart, Teubner (reprint 2012).

(1991) *La vita pitagorica* (ed. L. Deubner, 1937) with tr. It. M. Giangiullo, Milan, Rizzoli.

Lucretius, Titus Carus (1975) (*DRN*) *De rerum natura*, with tr. Eng. W. H. D Rouse, revised M. Ferguson Smith, Cambridge, MA and London, Harvard University Press and Heinemann.

Philostratus (2002) *Vite dei sofisti*, ed., comm. and tr. It., M. Civiletti, Milan, Bompiani.

Plato of Athens – references to dialogue title, page, division and line of H. Stephanus ed. 1578: where a modern apparatus or translation is cited, this is listed under 'Modern Authors'; title abbreviations adopted:

Euthyph.: *Euthyphro*
Cri.: *Crito*
Phd.: *Phaedo*
Tht.: *Theaetetus*
Phil.: *Philebus*
Sph.: *Sophist*
Pol.: *Statesman*
Prm: *Parmenides*
Smp.: *Symposium*
Phdr.: *Phaedrus*
Prt.: *Protagoras*
Grg: *Gorgias*
Resp.: *Republic*
Tim.: *Timaeus*
Epist.: *Letters*

Plutarch of Chaeronea (*Is. et Os.*,) *On Isis and Osiris*, in the Loeb *Moralia*, vol. V (1925) ed. and tr. F. C. Babbitt, Cambridge, MA, Harvard University Press.

(*Adv. Colot.*) *Against Colotes* in the Loeb *Moralia*, vol. XIV (1967) ed. and tr. B. Einarsson and P. De Lacey, Cambridge, MA, Harvard University Press.

Thomas Aquinas (*ST*: 1988) *Summa Theologiæ*, Cinisello Balsamo (MI), Edizioni Paoline.

Secondary Sources

Ackrill, J. L. (1965) 'Aristotle's Distinction between *Energeia* and *Kinesis*' in J. R. Bambrough (ed.), *New Essays on Plato and Aristotle*, London, Routledge and Kegan Paul, pp. 121–42.

Annas, J. (1999) *Platonic Ethics, Old and New*, Ithaca, Cornell University Press.

Anscombe, G. E. M. (1958) 'Modern Moral Philosophy' in her *Philosophical Papers* (3 vols.), Oxford, Basil Blackwell, 1981 III, pp. 26–42.

Aufderheide, J. (2020) *Aristotle's* Nicomachean Ethics *Book X: Translation and Commentary*, Cambridge, Cambridge University Press.

(2021) 'Eudoxus' Hedonism' in B. Sattler and U. Coope (eds.), *Ancient Ethics and the Natural World*, Cambridge, Cambridge University Press, pp. 185–202.

Barnes, J. (1980) 'Aristote chez les Anglophones', *Critique*, 36, pp. 705–18.

(1984) ed. *Revised Oxford Aristotle*, Oxford, Oxford University Press.

Barrett, S. P. (2004) 'The Hedonic Response to Cigarette Smoking Is Proportional to Dopamine Release in the Human Striatum as Measured by Positron Tomography and [11C]rarclopride', *Synapse*, 54, pp. 65–71.

Belshaw, C. (2014) 'What's Wrong with the Experience Machine', *European Journal of Philosophy*, 22, pp. 573–92.

Bencivenga, E. (1995) *Giocare per forza: Critica della società del divertimento*, Milan, Mondadori.

Bentham, J. (1823) *An Introduction to the Principles of Morals and Legislation*, J. H. Burns and H. L. A. Hart (eds.), Oxford, Oxford University Press (reprint 1970).

Berti, E. (1994) 'Il dibattito sul piacere nell'Accademia antica' in L. Montoneri (ed.), *I filosofi greci e il piacere*, Rome-Bari, Laterza, pp. 135–58.

Bett, R. (2020) 'Prodicus on the Choice of Heracles, Language and Religion' in D. C. Wolfsdorf (ed.), *Early Greek Ethics*, Oxford, Oxford University Press, pp. 195–220.

Bloom, P. (2010) *How Pleasure Works: The New Science of Why We Like What We Like*, London, Bodley Head.

Boileau, I. (2003) 'Alcohol Promotes Dopamine Release in the Human Nucleus Accumbens', *Synapse*, 49, pp. 226–31.

Botul, J.-B. (pseud.) (1999) *La vie sexuelle d'Emmanuel Kant*, Paris, Fayard.

Brandwood, L. (1992) 'Stylometry and Chronology' in R. Kraut (ed.), *Cambridge Companion to Plato*, Cambridge, Cambridge University Press, pp. 90–120.

Brunschwig, J. (1986) 'The Cradle Argument in Epicureanism and Stoicism' in M. Schofield and G. Striker (eds.), *The Norms of Nature*, Cambridge, Cambridge University Press, pp. 113–44.

Cajori, F. (1906) *A History of Mathematics* (2nd ed.), London, Macmillan.

Cheng, W. (2020) 'Aristotle and Eudoxus on the Argument from Contraries', *Archiv für Geschichte der Philosophie*, 102(4), pp. 588–618.

Connell, S. M. (2021) *Aristotle on Women*, Cambridge, Cambridge University Press.

Dancy, R. M. (1991) *Two Studies in the Early Academy*, Albany, State University of New York Press.

Davies, R. (2004) 'The Demon and the Scientist', *Epistemologia*, XXVII, pp. 299–318.

(2017) 'The Measure of Pleasure: A Note on the *Protagoras*', *Journal of the American Philosophical Association*, III, 3, pp. 301–15.

(2018) *Nietzsche disintossicato*, Milan, L'ornitorinco.

(2020) 'In Defence of a Fallacy', *Studia Semiotyczne*, XXXIV, 2, pp. 25–42.

De Santillana, G. (1940) 'Eudoxus and Plato: A Study in Chronology', *Isis*, 32, pp. 248–62.

Denyer, N. (2008) ed. and comm., *Plato: Protagoras*, Cambridge, Cambridge University Press.

Donner, W. (1998) 'Utilitarianism' in J. Skorupski (ed.), *The Cambridge Companion to Mill*, Cambridge, Cambridge University Press, pp. 254–92.

Fermani, A. (2008) tr. It. and comm., *Aristotele: Le tre etiche*, Milan, Bompiani.

Frede, D. (1992) 'Disintegration and Restoration: Pleasure and Pain in Plato's *Philebus*' in R. Kraut (ed.), *The Cambridge Companion to Plato*, Cambridge, Cambridge University Press, pp. 425–63.

Geach, P. T. (1960) 'Ascriptivism' reprinted in his *Logic Matters*, Oxford, Basil Blackwell, 1972, pp. 250–4.

Giannantoni, G. (1958) *I cirenaici*, Florence, Sansoni.

Gosling, J. C. B. (1975) ed. and comm., *Plato: Philebus*, Cambridge, Cambridge University Press.

Gosling, J. C. B. and C. C. W. Taylor (1982) *The Greeks on Pleasure*, Oxford, Clarendon Press.

Guthrie, W. K. C. (1978) *The Later Plato and the Academy* (vol. V of his *History of Greek Philosophy*), Cambridge, Cambridge University Press.

Gwyn Griffiths, J. (1965) 'A Translation from the Egyptian by Eudoxus', *Classical Quarterly*, 15, pp. 75–8.

Hacking, I. (1975) *The Emergence of Probability*, Cambridge, Cambridge University Press.

Harsanyi, J. (1986) 'Individual Utilities and Utilitarian Ethics' in A. Diekmann and P. Mitter (eds.), *Paradoxical Effects of Social Behavior: Essays in Honor of Anatol Rapoport*, Heidelberg-Vienna, Physica-Verlag, pp. 1–12.

(1995) *L'utilitarismo*, M. Piccone (ed. and tr.), Milan, Il saggiatore.

Harte, V. (2014) '*The Nicomachean Ethics* on Pleasure' in R. Polansky (ed.), *The Cambridge Companion to Aristotle's* Nicomachean Ethics, Cambridge, Cambridge University Press, pp. 288–318.

Heath, R. G. (1963), 'Electrical Self-Stimulation of the Brain in Man', *American Journal of Psychiatry*, 120, pp. 571–7.

Hume, D. (1777) *An Enquiry Concerning the Principles of Morals*, L. A. Selby-Bigge and (3rd ed. rev.) P. H. Nidditch (ed.), Oxford, Oxford University Press, 1975 (following the Selby-Bigge paragraph numbers).

Jones, H. (1989) *The Epicurean Tradition*, London, Routledge.

Kant, I. (1784) *Idea of a Universal History from a Cosmopolitan Point of View*, tr. Eng. L. Beck, Indianapolis, Bobbs-Merrill, 1963.

Karpp, H. (1933) *Untersuchungen zur Philosophie des Eudoxos von Knidos*, Würzburg-Aumühle, Triltsch.

Kenny, A. (1978) *The Aristotelian Ethics: A Study of the Relationship between the Eudemian and the Nicomachean Ethics of Aristotle*, Oxford, Clarendon.

Koepp, M. J. (1998) 'Evidence for Striatal Dopamine Release during a Video Game'. *Nature*, 393, pp. 366–8.

Kolata, G. (2008) 'Yes, Running Can Make You High', *The New York Times*, 27 March. www.nytimes.com/2008/03/27/health/nutrition/27best.html.

Kringelbach, M. L. (2007) 'Deep Brain Stimulation for Chronic Pain Investigated with Magnetoencephalography', *Neuroreport*, 8, pp. 223–8.

(2009) *The Pleasure Centre: Trust Your Animal Instincts*, Oxford, Oxford University Press.

Lamb, R. J. (1991) 'The Reinforcing and Subjective Effects of Morphine in Post-Addicts: A Dose-Response Study', *Journal of Pharmacology and Experimental Therapeutics*, 259, pp. 1165–73.

Leopardi, G. (1824) 'Dialogo di Torquato Tasso e del suo Genio familiare' in S. Orlando (ed.), *Operette Morali*, Rizzoli, Milan, 1976, pp. 142–50.

(1826) 'Dialogo di Cristoforo Colombo e di Pietro Gutierrez' in S. Orlando (ed.), *Operette Morali*, Rizzoli, Milan, 1976, pp. 224–8.

(1831) 'La quiete dopo la tempesta' in F. Brioschi (ed.), *Canti*, Rizzoli, Milan, 1974, pp. 139–40.

Lermontov, M. Yu. (1840) *Geroi Nashevo Vremeni* (*A Hero of Our Time*) D. J. Richards (ed.), Letchworth, Bradda Library of Russian Classics, 1962.

Martin, P. (2008) *Sex, Drugs and Chocolate: The Science of Pleasure*, London, Fourth Estate.

Merlan, P. (1960) 'Life of Eudoxus', appendix to his *Studies in Epicurus and Aristotle*, Wiesbaden, Otto Harrassowitz, pp. 98–104.

Migliori, M. (2000) *Filebo*, tr. It., intro. and comm., Milan, Bompiani.

Mill, J. S. (1861) 'Utilitarianism' in J. M. Robson, F. E. Priestley and D. P. Dryen (eds.), *The Collected Works of John Stuart Mill*, London, Routledge and Kegan Paul, 1968, Vol X.

Moore, G. E. (1903) *Principia Ethica*, Cambridge, Cambridge University Press.

Nietzsche, F. (1873) 'Ueber Wahrheit und Lüge im aussermoralischen Sinne' in G. Colli and M. Montinari (eds.), *Werke. Kritishche Gesamtausgabe* (15 vol.), Berlin and New York, 1973, vol. I, pp. 369–84.

Nikolsky, B. (2001) 'Epicurus on Pleasure', *Phronesis*, XLVI, pp. 440–65.

Nozick, R. (1974) *Anarchy, State and Utopia*, New York, Basic Books.

Olds, J. and Milner, P. (1954), 'Positive Reinforcement Produced by Electrical Stimulation of the Septal Area and Other Regions of Rat Brain', *Journal of Comparative and Physiological Psychology*, 47, pp. 419–27.

Palmer, A. (2014) *Reading Lucretius in the Renaissance*, Cambridge, MA, Harvard University Press.

Pascal, B. (1962) *Pensées*, L. Lafuma (ed.), Paris, Seuil.

Pirsig, R. M. (1974) *Zen and the Art of Motorcycle Maintenance*, New York, William Morrow.

Putnam, H. (1981) *Reason, Truth and History*, Cambridge, Cambridge University Press.

Rackham, H. (1934) *The Nicomachean Ethics*, ed. and tr. Eng., Cambridge, MA and London, Harvard University Press and Heinemann.

Radice, R. and Davies, R. (1997) *Aristotle's* Metaphysics: *Annotated Bibliography of the Twentieth-Century*, Leiden, Brill.

Reale, G. (1997) *Eros: dèmone mediatore*, Milan, Rizzoli.
  (2004) *Storia della filosofia greca e romana* (10 vol.), Milan, Bompiani.

Richardson, H. S. (1990) 'Measurement, Pleasure and Practical Science in Plato's *Protagoras*', *Journal of the History of Philosophy*, 28, pp. 7–32.

Ross, W. D. (1925) tr. Eng., *Ethica Nicomachea*, Oxford, Oxford University Press.

Russell, D. (2005) *Plato on Pleasure and the Good Life*, Oxford, Oxford University Press.

Ryle, G. (1954) *Dilemmas*, Cambridge, Cambridge University Press.

Schopenhauer, A. (1819) 'Das Welt als Wille und Vorstellung' in A. Hübscher (ed.), *Sämtliche Werke*, vol. 2 and 3, Wiesbaden, Brockhaus, 1972.

(1851) 'Parerga und Paralipomena' in A. Hübscher (ed.) vol. 5 and 6, *Sämtliche Werke*, Wiesbaden, Brockhaus, 1972.

Shakespeare, W. (1606) *The Tragedie of King Lear*, anastatic reprint of the First Folio, New York, Norton, 1996, pp. 791–817.

Shaw, J. C. (2015) *Plato's Anti-hedonism and the* Protagoras, Cambridge, Cambridge University Press.

Sidgwick, H. (1907) *The Methods of Ethics*, London, Macmillan.

Taub, L. (1998) 'Eudoxus of Cnidus' in E. J. Craig (ed.), *Routledge Encyclopedia of Philosophy*, London, Routledge, vol. 3, pp. 452–3.

Thomson, J. A. K. (1953) tr. Eng., *The Ethics of Aristotle*, London, Allen & Unwin.

Warren, J. (2009) 'Aristotle on Speusippus on Eudoxus on Pleasure' *Oxford Studies in Ancient Philosophy*, 36, pp. 249–81.

(2014) *The Pleasures of Reason in Plato, Aristotle and the Hellenistic Hedonists*, Cambridge, Cambridge University Press.

(2015) 'The Bloom of Youth', *Apeiron*, 48, pp. 327–45.

Weiss, R. (1979) 'Aristotle's Criticism of Eudoxan Hedonism' *Classical Philology*, 74, pp. 214–21.

West, H. R. (2004) *An Introduction to Mill's Utilitarian Ethics*, Cambridge, Cambridge University Press.

Wilson, C. (2009) 'Epicureanism in Early Modern Philosophy' in J. Warren (ed.), *The Cambridge Companion to Epicureanism*, Cambridge, Cambridge University Press, pp. 266–86.

Wodehouse, P. G. (1943) *Right Ho, Jeeves* reprinted in *Life with Jeeves*, Harmondsworth, Penguin, 1981, pp. 369–557.

Wolfsdorf, D. (2011) 'Prodicus on the Correctness of Names: The Case of τέρψις, χαρά and εὐφροσύνη', *Journal of Hellenic Studies*, 121, pp. 131–45.

Zanatta, M. (2008) ed. and tr. It. *Dialoghi di Aristotele*, Milan, Rizzoli.

Žižek, S. (2021) 'The Vagaries of the Superego' in *Elementa: Intersections between Philosophy, Epistemology and Empirical Perspectives* (1–2), pp. 13–31.

Acknowledgements

This Element is the residue of lecture courses held at the universities of Birmingham and Bergamo, so I am much indebted to the students who were patient with them, as well as to Nick Dent for encouraging my first outings in this direction. I am grateful to the late Giovanni Reale and to Roberto Radice of the Catholic University, Milan, for the opportunity to publish a summary version in Italian, and to Nick Denyer for challenging comments on that text. The present series editor, James Warren, has been both supportive and incisive in following the development of the work. As with everything I've done over the last thirty or so years, I dedicate the book to Alessandra Violi.

Cambridge Elements ☰

Ancient Philosophy

James Warren
University of Cambridge

James Warren is Professor of Ancient Philosophy at the University of Cambridge. He is the author of *Epicurus and Democritean Ethics* (Cambridge, 2002), *Facing Death: Epicurus and his Critics* (2004), *Presocratics* (2007) and *The Pleasures of Reason in Plato, Aristotle and the Hellenistic Hedonists* (Cambridge, 2014). He is also the editor of *The Cambridge Companion to Epicurus* (Cambridge, 2009), and joint editor of *Authors and Authorities in Ancient Philosophy* (Cambridge, 2018).

About the Series

The Elements in Ancient Philosophy series deals with a wide variety of topics and texts in ancient Greek and Roman philosophy, written by leading scholars in the field. Taking a theme, question, or type of argument, some Elements explore it across antiquity and beyond. Others look in detail at an ancient author, a specific work, or a part of a longer work, considering its structure, content, and significance, or explore more directly ancient perspectives on modern philosophical questions.

Cambridge Elements ≡

Ancient Philosophy

Elements in the Series

Printed in the United States
by Baker & Taylor Publisher Services